THE
KINDNESS
COLLECTION

Chuck Wall, Ph.D.

Kindness, Inc.
P. O. Box 3074
Bakersfield, California 93385

COVER DESIGN

The Kindness, Inc. logo, which is the heart-shaped globe of the world depicted on the front cover, was designed by Marti McAllister of Point Ventura, Texas.

ISBN 0-9654840-0-9
Printed in the United States of America.

This book is dedicated to my wife, Di, who has lived this book every day and every night. Every part of this project has Di's imprint upon it. Di's eyes and good judgment have guided this book through each stage of its development. Oh, and thanks to our Russian Blue cat, Star, for putting up with much disruption in her life as she rules our home with majestic authority.

ACKNOWLEDGMENTS

Putting together a book that is a collection of stories is not as easy as you may think. Some three years went into collecting and sorting stories for future reference. Hundreds had to be set aside to provide variety, while others had to be shortened to fit into a manageable book length.

My deepest thanks go to each person who has either sent me a story, or who has responded to my request to write his or her story when, in several cases, he or she didn't know there was a story to tell. This collection will be read with enjoyment because you were willing to share your lives with the rest of us. We all needed you to tell your story so we can reflect upon our own lives. Thanks to you, our lives are enriched.

This collection would not have happened had it not been for several dedicated professionals who put many hours of effort into selecting, editing, proofreading, computer entering, printing, and providing emotional support. Joan Swenson, columnist for The Bakersfield Californian newspaper, got the book started by offering to assist in the most difficult task of story selection. Joan then did the impossible. She took boxes of stories I had collected, put them into some semblance of order, and first-cut edited them, so I could determine if, in all that paper, we actually had a book.

It took the incredible skills of Janet Skibinski to fine tune each story into a living presentation for each of us to enjoy. Each story was given a title that represents what the story is about. Thanks, Janet, for great wit and humor. The many hours Joan and Janet spent writing and rewriting made this book come to life.

Curtis and Gail Istre took raw material and turned it into computerized excellence. I still am amazed at how these two could take our stories, pour them through a funnel into a computer, sort, spindle, and avoid mutilation, and present what you see on each page. Your skills are phenomenal.

Our friends, Greg and Patsy Randall, devoted many hours to reading stories out loud so we all could hear the message and spot grammatical errors as well as just plain enjoy positive thoughts. Thanks for being there P. and G.

Many others offered advice and counsel during the book's development stages. Fred Jacobs, Mike Russo, Craig O'Neill, Robie Lester Eccleston, Abbas Grammy and Sylvia O'Brien deserve special recognition.

HOW TO READ THIS BOOK

You are probably used to reading a book starting at the first page and reading to the end where you find out what you have been looking for but had to wait for the final conclusion on the last page. This is not that type of book.

Each story in this book is an island unto itself. The story before and the story after are different and, therefore, do not need to be read in order to understand the story you happen to be reading. Each story is true. Each author lived his or her experience. Each author wants you to feel what she or he felt at the time the story took place. Each of us, who wrote a story shown to you on these pages, believes you will benefit from our experiences and, perhaps, find an opportunity to commit an act of kindness similar to or vastly different from those we are sharing.

To thoroughly enjoy this book, start on any page. For those more traditional readers, start on page one and read cover to cover. One caution -- don't try to read this book in one sitting. You will find that you need to have time to absorb the meaning and implications of each story before moving to the next. One story before going to sleep may be just what you need to shed the troubles of the day and focus your attention on something uplifting, inspirational, and soothing.

There are about 100 stories for you to ponder. If you read one story per night, by the time you have finished the book, it's time to start again. Some of these stories are humorous, some are sad, and some are just plain ordinary. Each has been selected so you, the reader, can think about your own life in relation to what you have read.

Some may bring back memories of something you did that was particularly kind. Some may remind you of opportunities you had to be kind but failed to take advantage of the moments. Some you may do all the time and wonder why everyone else doesn't do them, also.

Whatever life experiences you bring to this book, we know you will benefit from the realization that most of us are trying our best to make our lives filled with respect and dignity. We want violence to end and believe the stories like you will read within these covers will help you enjoy life -- one story at a time.

ABOUT THE AUTHOR

Chuck Wall was born January 12, 1941, in Los Angeles, California. He was raised in Bakersfield, where he currently lives and is a Professor of Human Relations and Management at Bakersfield College. Chuck holds a B.A. in Business Administration and an M.B.A. in Management/Marketing and Group Dynamics, both from San Francisco State University. He earned a Ph.D. in Educational Administration and Marketing Management from the University of California, Los Angeles.

His incredible and varied life experiences include co-authoring a book on organizational renewal, producing a multi-media look into the 21st century for a White House conference, hosting his own television and radio programs, and most recently, with the Stroud Puppets, publishing a five-act video program entitled "Kindness for Kids." Dr. Wall has headed two of his own firms, one in publishing, and one in manufacturing. He was the signature speaker for the Million Dollar Round Table Conference in 1994, pulpit guest of Dr. Robert Schuller at the Crystal Cathedral in October, 1994, and in March, 1995, was awarded the Hero of Peace Award for North America by Discovery Toys.

Married to his own "Princess Di" for 32 years, they have formed a finely coordinated team with Di providing the organization that enables Chuck to pursue his many interests. These include business and industry in our global community as well as his career and his crusade for Kindness. Even though he is blind, Chuck does not consider himself disabled, but merely must spend extra time dealing with one of life's little nuisances.

THE KINDNESS STORY

Alternately, I have been blessed and condemned for creating the sentence, "Commit a random act of kindness." Here is the truth - *I DID NOT* create this phrase, but I may well be responsible for what is now a worldwide movement! There are references to random acts of kindness in literature going back centuries. I am going to tell you how it happened for me, because it has changed my life...for the better, I might add.

It began in early September, 1993. I was having breakfast and listening to the news on the radio. (I never *just* listen to the radio; I am always off thinking about something else. My mind seems to work like the first line of a poem I once heard, "Each thing I do, I rush through, so I can do something else.") So, while listening to the news, I was also thinking about something different to engage the minds of my Human Relations and Motivation students at Bakersfield College. What could I do that I hadn't done already?

Since the news is rarely uplifting, I was only vaguely aware of the newscaster's comments until he dramatically proclaimed, "Ladies and gentlemen, today we have another random act of senseless violence to report." My immediate reaction was one of anger. *VIOLENCE, VIOLENCE!* Is that all we can talk about these days? Isn't there anything else that can hold our attention besides another random act of senseless violence?

As I began to calm down, I started the process of word association. What is in that phrase that I might use to launch an assignment for my students? What if I took out "violence" and inserted *kindness*? What I had then was, "Ladies and gentlemen, today we have another random act of senseless kindness to report." (I wondered if that phrase would ever appear in a newscast in my lifetime, and decided the chances were about the same as the lottery odds!) However, I had the elusive assignment for my class.

I walked into my 9 a.m. Human Relations class, instructed the students to take out paper and pen, and to write down the following, "Today, I will go out into the community and commit one random act of senseless...," and at this point I waited for them to catch up..."*kindness.*" I got the usual questions. Is this going to count toward our grades, and how much is it worth? Does the paper have to be typed? What's a kindness? Give us *your* definition.

I answered all questions except the last. I didn't want them to write about what they thought *I* believed to be kindness, but, rather, what *they* thought kindness meant. "This assignment is due in two weeks. Happy hunting!" I said. Had I been more specific, the students would not have shown the variety of ideas they were capable of generating. What happened is now a part of the kindness story history, but, more importantly, what we now have is a look into our future.

Here are just a few glimpses of their efforts. You will read about some of them in greater detail in this collection. One woman took her daughter to visit patients in a convalescent hospital, one gave up her parking space in a full lot, and another found a stray collie and, with creative effort, located the owner. A young man paid his mother's electric bill with money he earned during the summer. One male student paid for a woman's lunch while in line at the college cafeteria (this one almost backfired!). And two students took furry, stuffed animals to the children's ward of a local hospital.

While this was meant to be just an assignment to be turned in for a grade, that's not the way it worked. One of the students, Jo Marshall, without my knowledge, contacted a reporter from the local newspaper, The Bakersfield Californian. Jo thought this might make a good story. The reporter, Liz Barker, went to her editor, told him about it, and asked if he thought it was worth covering. He left it up to her. Rather than come to my office in person, Liz called a very surprised me and conducted a less than enthusiastic interview by telephone.

After she had time to think about it, the assignment I had given didn't seem so kooky afterall. In fact, the article ran on the front page of the Saturday edition. The class and I were pleased with the newspaper's coverage of a *good* news story, and enjoyed the attention we received for a few days. Within a week, we were on to the next assignment and all was forgotten except the newspaper clipping.

Then I received another telephone call. This time it was from Nancy Mayer, a reporter for <u>The Associated Press</u>. She came across the kindness article while perusing newspaper stories from Central California. She asked if she could come to Bakersfield for a day to interview me and get the reactions regarding this assignment from my students. At the end of the following week, Nancy had her story, but she warned me not to get my hopes up. Frequently, stories just seem to die somewhere in the system.

Nearly three weeks had gone by and the interview was becoming a dim memory. Then on Friday of the third week, Nancy called. "You may want to get ready. The editors in New York have decided to run the story on the wire and send it to every radio and television station and every newspaper they are associated with around the world! You might get a phone call or two." The next week the story ran in about 1,000 newspapers, on television news shows and radio programs.

We didn't get a few phone calls - we got thousands! We lost track of the calls when the switchboard at Bakersfield College was jammed for several days. Interview requests poured in and I found myself doing five or six radio programs per day, often starting at 5:00 a.m. and doing all night shows on the East Coast. Charles Osgood of CBS radio did an *Osgood File* report. Then the mail started arriving. First by 10 or 20, then by the hundreds of letters each day, for months on end!

The Crusaders television program spent a week with us in November, 1993. The audience response was so great from this episode that a follow-up segment was immediately planned. It involved me talking with a group of teenagers who had recently experienced a random act of senseless violence. Some of their parents were aboard the Long Island commuter train in which a gunman randomly opened fire. I began by asking them to tell me about themselves - where they live, about their parents, brothers and sisters, their high school activities, their hopes and dreams for the future. Together we began to plan community activities in which they could become involved. The objective was to see if by becoming involved in others lives, they might turn their pain and anger regarding this act of violence away from their need for vengeance and toward the realization that their energies might be used positively in other areas.

Another shift in our lives came from that trip to New York. A United States Congressman, Walter Tucker (D-California), contacted *The Crusaders* to say he wanted to introduce a congressional resolution to the House of

Representatives, declaring one week each year as "Kindness Awareness Week." *The Crusaders* staff put his legislative assistant in touch with me and we began developing the wording for the resolution. When asked what week I thought would be best for this national celebration, I suggested the week of Feb. 14. The week was accepted, presented to Congress, and received a unanimous "*YES*" vote on the floor of the House of Representatives. At the conclusion of this collection, you will find a copy of the original resolution Congressman Tucker circulated among his colleagues.

At the same time, the State Caucus Chair from Pennsylvania contacted me to collaborate on the wording of a Pennsylvania state resolution. This was the first of many states to declare kindness awareness days and weeks.

CNN came to my classroom and aired a story that went around the world. Now calls were coming from Russia, England, France, Sweden, Germany, Canada, and Puerto Rico. But the most memorable came from Doris Bacon, a reporter for <u>People</u> magazine. She scheduled a day to spend with my class and discover what all the fuss was about. Her article was published in the Dec. 13, 1993, issue. I remember this clearly because on the front cover of the magazine was a picture of Lorena Bobbitt and her knife. Actually, my story followed hers, and, as my wife, Di, pointed out, it was better to be *after* Mrs. Bobbitt, than for Mrs. Bobbitt to be after me!

Appearing on *The Oprah Winfrey Show* in February, 1994, and as a guest of Dr. Robert Schuller, at the Crystal Cathedral during his *Hour of Power*, has brought the message of kindness to people in 100 countries. The challenge to commit a random act of kindness has touched 40 million people in the United States alone. Those who work hard to improve their communities, wherever that might be, are often lost in the dust of those getting attention by destroying our American way of life. Is it the fault of our government, our church, our schools? No, it is your fault and mine for *allowing* this to happen. We *can* solve the problem, and it really isn't that difficult. Just begin the process in your own home, school, church, and community. Treat others the way you want to be treated. Respect and dignity guide each of us to a solution for our nation's violence. Will this solve all of our problems? Not at all, but respect and dignity will go a long way to divert attention *away* from violence and *toward* kindness.

When we began our kindness assignment, my students suggested I create something that would help people remember what they were trying to do. They suggested a bumper sticker which is now seen around the world and has been printed on more than 50,000 stickers. The kindness phrase also appears on T-shirts.

Many of the stories in this book are those that people just like you have performed without the need for recognition. As you read, you may find the inspiration to do something positive for others around you. I challenge each of you: "Today, I will commit one random act of senseless KINDNESS... *Will You*?

Meat(ing) the Challenge

I t was 4 p.m. on Christmas Eve. The line at the supermarket was long and moving slowly. I had bought a 16-pound prime rib roast as a special treat for my family's Christmas dinner. My expertise with cooking prime rib roasts stopped at about 8 pounds and I was skeptical of my friend's "foolproof" recipe. She said to preheat the oven to 375 degrees, put in any size roast, cook it for one hour, turn off the heat, and do not open the oven door. Then 45 minutes before serving, turn the oven on to 300 degrees for 43 minutes to finish the cooking. Voila! A perfect prime rib roast!

As I stood in line concerned that the roast might still be pretty much uncooked if I used this method, and thinking of the 18 people waiting to eat it, I glanced into the shopping basket of the lady behind me. She had *two* of these big roasts in her cart. I remarked she must be expecting a lot of people for Christmas dinner. She replied, "Oh, no, my husband just likes prime rib." When I asked her how she planned to cook them, she said she had no idea what to do with them. Her husband was a chef and he would do the cooking.

When I revealed my cooking strategy, she had a rather worried look on her face. "I am not a cook, but I am involved with food handling and you might have a real problem with the meat spoiling," she cautioned.

Seeing my disappointed look, she said, "Let me talk to my husband. I'm sure he'll be glad to tell you what to do. Give me your name and phone number and I'll have him call you this evening when he gets home from work."

Sure enough, about 8 p.m. on Christmas Eve the call came. This very nice man, who had never laid eyes on me, spent about 15 minutes of his precious Christmas Eve telling a total stranger how to cook meat for her Christmas dinner. What a special touch of the Christmas spirit!

When he finished giving me the instructions and making sure I understood them, he said, "There is just one thing I want to ask of you. The next time someone else has a need and you can help, pass on this same kind of help to him or her." I assured him I would, thanked him profusely, and wished him a very Merry Christmas.

The prime rib was out of this world! And what a joy it was to receive such a special act of kindness.

--Jeanne Swigart

Out of the Mouths of Babes

One afternoon I was sitting on our family room couch feeling very upset and depressed. I couldn't shake myself out of this awful feeling. I just sat there staring into space, wishing and praying that I could find a way to make myself feel better.

It was at that moment that my 3-year-old daughter, Julia, came up to me and said, "Mommy, are you sad?" "Yes," I responded. "You do this," and mirroring my expression, she lowered her chin to her chest and frowned.

Slowly lifting her head until her eyes were even with mine, the biggest, warmest smile appeared on her face. Looking up at me, she asked with all the enthusiasm she had, "Where's your happy face?" I began to laugh as I heard my little girl repeat to me what I had said to her so many times before when she was upset.

Now *she* was making *me* feel better! When Julia saw me laughing, she cheered, "There it is!" And there it was!

--Gretchen Penner

Love, The Source of All Power

J ose, a young man of 19, overheard his mother talking to a friend on the telephone one September afternoon. His mother was confiding to her friend that the electric bill was due and she didn't know where the money was coming from to pay it. She was afraid the electricity would be turned off.

Jose had worked hard during the summer and was back in college. He had saved his money, and without saying a word to his mother, took the electric bill, withdrew the money from his account, and paid the bill. That night at the dinner table, he presented the paid receipt to his mother. Not only was Jose's mother surprised and grateful for what he had done, but she was extremely proud of her son's true act of kindness.

A Lingering Smile

I n the 1960's, a television commercial aired featuring a "white knight" who rescued housewives from the dirtiest of dirt. During that same time, I was an active member of the Indian Wells Valley Search and Rescue Team (IWVSR).

A few days before Thanksgiving 1967, the IWVSR received an emergency call concerning an airplane that had slammed into the eastern side of the Sierra Nevada mountain range, between Owens Peak and Olancha Peak. Within a short time, we had assembled and began the arduous climb toward the crash site. It was a long, rugged, steep journey through rain, snow, terrible cold and blowing wind and, to compound matters, it was dark!

When we arrived at the crash site, the plane appeared to be intact but badly ripped up. Moments later, I was extracting the limp body of the front passenger, a little girl about 10 years old. The pilot, who was also dead, was removed next. In the back of the airplane were two more people; they were the wife and teenage daughter of the pilot and they were still alive!

When a helicopter from nearby China Lake arrived sometime later, we placed the wife on a stretcher, carried her to the helicopter, and secured the stretcher in place. She was in great pain from many broken bones and badly mangled feet and ankles. As I was leaving the helicopter, she took my hand and told me how much she appreciated my efforts. The memory of her sincere smile at that moment is one that has stayed with me for nearly 30 years and one I recall almost everyday.

The IWVSR received a letter from the woman several months later stating she and her daughter had survived the ordeal. She said her husband had been the "white knight" from the television commercial.

--Gerald Brown

I let my sister sit in the front seat of the car. I helped clean up at Girl Scouts. I erased the board for my teacher. I told my friend, Kenza, that she was a great person. I got everyone in my class a Valentine's gift. I helped my grandma find cool stuff at Panama Smithsonian. I read to a little first grader. I told my sister I loved her instead of fighting back.

--Kathryn, age 9

Kindness Knows No Bounds

O ne cold winter day, I was driving down two-lane Highway 126 in Ventura County, California, heading toward the little town of Santa Paula. As I drove along, I noticed something in the road which appeared to be a large rat, directly in the path of my car. I couldn't see its head since it was laying on its back with its neck distended away from me, but I thought I detected a twitch. The possibility of it being crushed by the next car that came along was a certainty, and I felt even a rat deserved better than to be smashed as it lay helpless to do anything.

I quickly parked my car and ran over to the animal with the intention of using my boot to nudge it off the road onto the shoulder. To my shock, I realized it was a small dachshund, lying with its eyes open, but obviously alive. I gently scooped it up and rushed to find a veterinarian, some five miles away.

After finding three vets closed for lunch, I was able to contact one whose nurse told me he was next door having lunch. I asked that he come to the office at once. When the doctor looked at the little dog, he said she had suffered a traumatic injury to her spine and that she probably would not survive. He suggested I leave her with him.

I checked on the dog daily, and at the end of four days, the veterinarian called me and suggested I pick the dog up. He felt she would either die or be paralyzed for life and he wanted her to be home with us when it happened.

We put her in a box with high sides, and put the box in a small area. We had been warned to keep her as still as possible. We left food and water for her and petted her until she fell asleep.

The next morning, to our surprise, we found she had pulled herself over the top of the box and was lying on the floor beside it. We took her to our room to watch her more carefully. She seemed to improve and developed a healthy appetite. After three days, the little dog took a gigantic leap and jumped onto our bed. Her recovery was nothing short of miraculous, and to this day, she can outrun our smaller dogs and even our two larger dogs.

Perhaps, it was an act of kindness on my part to pick up a little dog off a cold highway. But, to me, it was her act of kindness, because she brought her love and affectionate spirit to our home as her gift and way of saying "thank you."

--Robie Lester Eccleston

Staking A Claim On Kindness

S ometimes finding an empty parking place in a mall parking lot is about as easy as finding gold nuggets in a dry river bed. Jessica shared her experience involving driving around and around looking for that one space that everyone else had missed.

Excitement rose as she spotted an empty space ahead, only to discover a motorcycle tucked in between two vans. Finally, she found it, the spot no one else had seen!

"As I drove into the parking spot," she said, "and began to turn off the engine, I looked in my rear view mirror to see a woman stop just behind me, obviously thinking she would get the spot but seeing I had already staked claim to it." The woman threw her hands up in sheer frustration.

As Jessica observed this behavior, and knowing what the woman was thinking, Jessica did the unimaginable. She put her car in reverse, backed out of the space, and waved the woman into it. The woman looked at her, mouth agape, not believing what was taking place and knowing this never happens in real life!

"Once the woman realized I was serious," Jessica said, "she quickly drove into the space before I changed my mind." Jessica had to park about a quarter mile away from her destination, but she felt so good just knowing she had made the woman's day, she smiled the whole day.

I was willing to split my Ding Dong with my little brother, Daniel. I shared my chicken nuggets with my friends. I bought Daniel his stuffed rabbit. I gave my teacher, Ms. McBean, a free necklace. I read Daniel a story. I signed up to be a buddy or a hugger in the Special Olympics. I baby-sat Daniel for free. I agreed to baby-sit instead of have a sleepover. This is just one-fifth of what I did.

--Pamela, age 8

It's About Time

At age 44, I abandoned the corporate ship, relocated to a small, mountain town, and set out to do what I really love: clock repair. A recent encounter with an elderly customer provides a perfect example of the daily potential for satisfaction.

Martha called and tried to explain the problem with her clock, but the years had ravaged her voice and it was all I could do to get just her name and address. She lived in the older part of town in a tiny little house with a creaky gate out front. Her daughter let me in and escorted me to Martha's bedroom, which hardly qualified as such since there was barely room for the furniture it contained: a bed, a 13-inch TV, and the chair in which Martha sat.

Upon seeing me, Martha's face lit up with a big smile. I suspect she was thrilled just to have anybody visit, but especially somebody who could restore her precious clock back to working condition. It sat there on the television, a humpback or tambour style from the 1920's, with its original works replaced at some time with a simple electric movement.

It became clear after a few minutes that her room, her TV, and her clock were the focal points of her daily life. Moving around the house was very difficult, so she just spent most days in her room. The clock had been given to her by her mother, and she needed it not only to schedule her TV programs, but to "keep punctual about things." I doubt there was much left in her life to be on time for, but as one who also has a great respect for time, I knew well how she felt. When I told Martha it would take a couple of weeks to repair her clock, she was most distressed. "That long," she said with a forlorn look.

It was at that moment I decided if ever there was a need for a random act of senseless kindness, this was it. Instead of the usual two weeks and $50 (not to mention $40 for the two house calls) that would be normal for such a job, I wanted to tell her I'd do it for nothing as fast as I could. By now, though, I knew Martha would never accept charity, so I told her $20 and six days. She seemed a little suspicious of the low price, but I assured her that was all I would charge anybody under the circumstances - which is true.

I drove home, immediately special ordered a brand new movement with one-day delivery, installed it within hours of arrival, polished the case to a high luster, and got it back to Martha in two days flat! It was a furious effort, but the light in Martha's eyes at seeing her beautiful clock back on its television throne so quickly made it all worth it. I'm not sure Martha even knew an act of kindness had been committed, but I do, and I'll tell you, it is one fantastic feeling!

--Greg Randall

The Snowball Effect

For a long time, my neighbor needed his car washed, and a little wax wasn't going to hurt it either. My neighbor works nights and sleeps during the day, so he doesn't have much time to do other things.

One morning, when I knew he was asleep, I went over to his house and washed and waxed his car. I had a lot of fun doing it and I knew that he would be very happy. When I finished, I stuck the bumper sticker I got from Dr. Wall under his windshield wiper. It reads, "Today I will commit one random act of senseless KINDNESS... *Will You?*"

The next day, my neighbor asked if I knew who washed his car. I felt if I told him, it wouldn't be a senseless kindness. I didn't want him to try to repay me some day by washing my truck. I would rather he commit an act of senseless kindness himself.

Well, it worked. Other neighbors of ours had sod delivered to their home because there was no grass in their backyard. My neighbor laid it out for them before they got home from work. When he was finished, he put the same bumper sticker I had given him into the flower bed. That neighbor was just as surprised as he had been.

My definition of senseless kindness is when you do something for someone and don't expect anything in return. I hoped my act of kindness would help others to see that it doesn't hurt to be nice and help someone out who needs it.

--Tony Capdeville

Our teacher, Mrs. Gallagher, put the (kindness) bumper sticker on her car. It looked nice. Teacher said she never put a bumper sticker on her car, none of them. Because they're not important, but that one was important to her and to us, too.

--Sonia, age 7

A Bag Lady of a Different Sort

When I went shopping with my mother at a store where you bag your own groceries, I decided to help people bag their purchases. First, I asked the manager for permission; he just laughed and said it was okay.

I started toward the cash registers. One middle-aged woman with tons of groceries gave me a nasty look and said, "No, I can do it by myself" when I offered to help. It was a bad start but that was not going to stop me.

For about five minutes I continued to ask other people if I could help with no success. Despite the nasty looks and comments I received, a mother of four made me forget all of it.

"Can I help you bag your groceries?" I asked her. She absent-mindedly said "yes." But as soon as she realized what I was doing, it seemed as though she could not stop smiling.

Committing a random act of senseless kindness can be tough and embarrassing. There were people who said "no" in a mean way, and there were people staring at me like I was going insane. But those who smiled and thanked me made the kindness worth doing.

--Vicki Yin

Delivering Kindness

My son, who is in the Army and stationed at Fort Hood, Texas, was on his way home to Bakersfield with his wife and two small sons for a visit. Five hours into their journey, my son took his eyes off the road to retrieve a cup from the car floor. He lost control of the car, overcorrected, and sent the vehicle into a frightening spin which landed them in the center median, facing the wrong way. No one was injured, but the front tires had blown out.

Luckily for them, a kind-hearted trucker saw what happened and stopped to see what he could do. This angel in overalls loaded everyone and the tires into his truck, drove them to the nearest town and waited while the rims were checked and the tires replaced. He drove them back to their car and helped my son put the new tires on.

My son couldn't stop singing this generous man's praises. He repeated over and over to me, "Mom, he did all this for us and he never asked for anything in return. I don't know what we would have done if he hadn't stopped."

Thanks to this man's kindness, we enjoyed a wonderful visit with my son and his family. But more importantly, it taught us all to think twice before passing a stranded stranger on a hot, dusty highway.

--Janet Skibinski

A Blooming Surprise

G ayle Morgan had never seen the gentleman who walked into the florist shop where she works. "How much is a bouquet of flowers?" he asked. "Well, that depends on the type of flowers, the size of the bouquet, and the vase," Gayle replied.

After pondering this information for a few minutes, the man told Gayle he wanted to spend $25. "Can you make something up that will be nice for that amount of money?" he asked. "Sure," Gayle said, as she reached for the order pad. "Would you like to take it with you, or do you want us to deliver it for you?"

"Deliver it," the man answered. "Fine. What is the name and address of the person you want to receive the flowers," Gayle asked. The gentleman then asked for a phone book and instructed Gayle to drop the book on its spine on the counter and "let it open by itself."

A bit perplexed, Gayle did as he requested. The book opened to a page about in the middle. The man then turned the phone book around so he could read the names and pointed to one at random. "This is the person I want the flowers delivered to," he said. "Is this someone you know?" Gayle asked. "No, I just want to commit a random act of kindness anonymously. These flowers are sure to brighten someone's day. Put a little note with the flowers saying, 'Just thought you would like your day brightened. Have a great day!'

Dear Dr. Wall:

We have a bulletin board in our class and we put our acts of kindness on a heart and hang them up. I appreciated you taking the time off work and coming to our class. I think it was a good idea for your class to do acts of kindness.

Love always,
Bonita, age 9

The Gift of Life

M ike Stier, owner of Stier's RV Sales in Bakersfield, California, knows what kindness is all about. Soon after the first story about my classroom assignment on kindness appeared in the newspaper, he phoned me and told me to have 3,000 bumper stickers printed and send the bill to him. He has a campaign of kindness of his own, to encourage people to donate their organs when they die. One Thanksgiving, he sent a letter, plus information about organ donation, to his employees. What follows are some excerpts.

"I've always believed in organ donation, but when the opportunity arose in my family, I was unsure of what to do until it was too late. My mother was 52 years old when a stroke left her brain dead. Once all the tests proved there was zero chance of recovery, life support machines were removed and she was allowed to die. The tragedy of my mom's death was unavoidable. The tragedy of not giving the gift of life to others through organ transplant, however, could have been. My mother had no further use for all those wonderfully healthy organs in her body and they could have meant life for many others.

"I encourage all of you to read this information about organ donation. I then encourage you to become involved to whatever extent you are comfortable and also to share this information with others."

Mike himself carries an organ donor card and said that as a result of his information campaign among his employees, many others have now become potential donors.

The "Look" of Kindness

My husband, George, and I were on our way home from several days of fishing and were now looking forward to showers, shaving, clean clothes and iced tea. We had come several miles through a rocky landscape when our scruffy little car stopped running. George discovered that we had been driving with a fan belt that had been waiting for any excuse to break.

We stood at the side of the road trying to flag someone down. A car drew to a stop some distance past us on the roadway. The occupants just sat there with the engine running. They did not look like ideal rescuers. As I recall, they were wearing black leather and there were motorcycle helmets in the back window. I wanted that particular car to move on.

After several silent minutes, the car started backing slowly towards us. My apprehension burst into full blown visions of mayhem. The car parked some distance from us. After a few moments, the driver got out of the car, and watching us intently, silently approached.

Well, not only did this driver give us a ride, but he and his wife went out of their way to deliver us to our front door. During the drive, they told us about the church motorcycle group they belonged to that had just enjoyed an outing. But that's not the twist that keeps this act of kindness clear and dear to my heart.

On the trip down that mountain, our saviors confessed. The reason for the several silent minutes parked just ahead of us along the road, and the cautious approach of the young husband while his wife waited in the car with the engine running, was their apprehensiveness approaching any couple who looked as bad as we did!

Kindness isn't always easy, but we were, and are, grateful that these young people took the extra time needed to determine that, at least in this one instance, it was safe to offer assistance to the unclean, unwashed and unshaven.

--Sandy Larson

Cleaning Up - His Act

B ill, a retired man who starts his day with a three-mile trek on a walking path near his home, was frustrated to see new graffiti showing up the beginning of each week. The concrete, park benches, monuments and just about any other surface that would hold spray paint was covered with it. Instead of waiting for the city to do something about it, Bill called the City Parks Department.

He asked if it would be okay for him to repaint the park benches and clean the spray paint off the light poles. The city officials were delighted. They even supplied Bill with paint brushes, paint and other supplies needed to complete the job.

"I'm sure they thought I was just mad," Bill said, "and would just go out just once and that would be the end."

But he has been cleaning graffiti for about three years without fanfare. I asked Bill if anyone said anything to him while he did his work. Lots of people stop and thank him, Bill said. Their pleasure in seeing the clean-up is what keeps him coming back, he explained.

Thanks, Bill, we all applaud your community spirit!

The Dress Makes the Woman

A couple of years ago, I bought a beautiful, floral-print, cotton dress of vivid colors - hot pink and teal green on a white background. It had a high neck in front, but dipped to a "V" in back. I loved it, but after trying it on several times at home, it was very evident that it was made for a younger woman. I decided to give it to someone who would like it as much as I did.

A few weeks ago, I was in church when I noticed a very pretty dark-haired and dark-eyed woman sitting several rows in front of me. The minute I saw her, I thought, "That dress would look beautiful on her."

After the service, I introduced myself to her and told her I had a beautiful dress that I would like to give her. She looked at me rather strangely, so I explained why I had the dress and how long I had been looking for the perfect person to whom to give it. She smiled and said she would be happy to have it. She told me she lived alone and worked at Taco Bell.

My husband and I took her to our home and I showed her the dress. She loved it! She tried it on and it fit like it was made for her. The colors were beautiful on her. She was so happy. We decided to celebrate and took her to lunch and then back to church where she had left her bicycle.

The next Sunday, she very proudly walked into church wearing "the dress." She looked lovely. She was just glowing. As she sat down beside me, a woman behind us said to her husband, "Oh, what a beautiful dress." That made both of us happy. She had a new dress and I knew it had found a new home.

--Doris Wolfe

Four Hands Are Better Than Two

One day I was in line at Burger King, along with several other people at lunch time. A woman was in front of me with a bazillion little kids. It was as if she had decided to take all the kids in her neighborhood out to lunch!

Naturally all the kids wanted something different to eat and drink, so the order took awhile. When the kids were finished ordering, they ran outside to the playground, leaving the woman with the task of filling their drink requests.

While I was waiting for my order, her number was called once, then twice. She was still filling the drinks and putting lids on them. Seeing that she obviously needed assistance, I asked if I could get the tray for her. She gave me a hesitant, "That would be great," and glanced around quickly, looking for the camera. I told her if she would show me where she was sitting, I would bring the drinks to her table. "Gee, that would be wonderful," was her response. When I set the tray down, I wished her a good day and went on my way.

As I was eating lunch with my friends, the woman gave me several big "Thank you" smiles. It gave me a good feeling and it was easy to do. There was no materialistic gain from it; she simply needed help and I offered it to her. I think it made both of our days.

As I reflect on this incident, I truly believe that if we all did one random act of kindness for one another, this would be a much better place to live. There are people out there that are willing to help, but you have to let them. It kind of helps you keep the faith.

--Ryan Olnick

Daisies That Delight

I wanted to do something that would last in someone's heart. I baked a dozen chocolate chip cookies and bought three daisies ready to be planted. Then I knocked on the elderly lady's door who lives across the street from me.

Without hesitation, she invited me in. "I have brought a gift for you. I hope you enjoy watching them grow," I said. I planted the daisies in her backyard. After I was done, I thanked her for welcoming me into her home. We talked for awhile and I could tell she didn't have visitors often. As I left, she thanked me and asked me to come again soon.

I am really surprised how this act of kindness had a positive impact on me. Today I won't hesitate to go out and commit at least one random act of senseless kindness.

--Rosa Ventura

The Kindness Song

A couple of years ago, Robie Lester Eccleston saw me being interviewed on a Los Angeles television program and was inspired to commit her own act of kindness. Robie decided to write a song about kindness, which is now our international theme song. It turns out that Robie is an ASCAP writer and publisher. If you, Dear Reader, are interested in the sheet music, please send us a self-addressed, stamped business-size envelope. Here is Robie's song.

A RANDOM ACT OF KINDNESS

If the world seems dark and gloomy,
I get out of bed and say
I can change the way it looks and see it
In a different way.

I can make the sun shine brightly
Even through a cloudy sky
And turn a tear
To a Thank You Dear
In the twinkling of an eye.

It's kind of a magic thing
But there's really nothing to it
Just make up your mind
That you'll be kind
And then go out and DO IT.

A Random Act of Kindness
Look around and you will see
That it's time you thought of the YOU YOU YOU
And forgot the me me me.

It can be very small
Or even as big as an ELEPHANT
So long as a Senseless Kindness is Committed
Then that's SWELL-A-PHANT.

A Random Act of Kindness
Doesn't cost a thing, it's free
It can make the world we live in,
A WONDERFUL PLACE
A WONDERFUL PLACE
A WON-DER-FUL PLACE--TO BE!

Picture Perfect

What is it that most amateur photographers never see in their pictures? Themselves!

Years ago, when I had a fortune invested in cameras and equipment and took pictures everywhere we went, I discovered something unusual. I had pictures of my wife, my children, my friends, my co-workers, and even strangers, but I had very few pictures of me. Why? Because I was always the one *taking* the picture.

From then until now, whenever I see a young man taking a picture of his young lady in front of a special scene he wants to remember, I volunteer to take a picture of both of them. Over the years, I've especially enjoyed taking pictures of foreign visitors we've encountered at Yellowstone, the Grand Tetons, Grand Canyon, Yosemite, Mount Rushmore--where ever there's a group wanting to have a memorable snapshot. My offer is always answered with the universal thank-you smile.

If you're looking for a simple random act of kindness that takes little time or effort, try being the "relief" photographer for the one who's never in the picture.

--Don Rodewald

Lassie, Where's Home?

For several days, Lisa had watched a disheveled collie wander her small mountain community neighborhood. Eventually, she was able to coax the dog into following her home where she fed it, gave it a bath, and groomed the burrs from it's coat.

As much as she would have liked to keep the collie, she knew that someone must be missing it. But what would be the best way to find the owner? Lisa hit upon an idea that was truly an act of kindness.

After taking pictures of the collie, she had them enlarged to poster-size and wrote on the posters, "If this is your dog, call..." Lisa hung the posters in laundromats, shopping centers, schools, and churches. It wasn't long until the owner phoned and the two were reunited. The owner said his attempts to find the dog had been futile until he saw one of the posters. A simple act of kindness put a smile on a man's face and a wag in the tail of his best friend.

...He's My Brother

The person I helped was not a stranger. He was my older brother, Ramon. Ramon has Down's Syndrome as well as other health problems that have made him weak and inactive. Despite all, he continues to be a cheerful person with high hopes.

One of Ramon's favorite sports is basketball. So early one Saturday morning, I asked him if he wanted to play a little one-on-one. I knew he would benefit from the exercise and we would enjoy spending the time together. We played for about an hour and had a great time filled with laughter.

That day I saw the greatest tenderness in his heart. He gave me plenty of thanks, not through his words but through his expressions. Ramon allowed me to feel how kindness comes to those who volunteer their kindness.

--Leticia Arguello

Ministering to the Ministers

While at a summer church retreat, I overheard my pastor's wife make a comment about how she never seemed to be able to get certain parts of the housework done and how she and her husband hadn't had time alone in years. Eager to do something special for them, who unselfishly provide their time and energy to others constantly, I wondered how to accomplish it without their knowledge.

I spoke with my daughter who agreed it would be a job for more than one person. Within an hour of calling people, my daughter's home was filled with parishioners willing to help. The ideas poured forth, a list of things to be done was made, and the work was broken into small jobs. The dilemma of doing it without their knowledge was quickly solved. Someone offered to care for their two small children while we sent our ministers on a weekend trip to the coast.

Needless to say, when the day came to send our pastors on their get-away, they were thrilled. We started to work immediately - washing windows inside and out, cleaning the refrigerator, washing and ironing the laundry, and cleaning and organizing the cupboards. Outside, the yard was manicured to perfection! When our pastors returned home, we were all there to greet them with our gift of love.

--Linda Austin

Giving Friends

O n June 7, 1996, I received some really devastating news. My friend's mom told me that my friend had been shot at a party that I had just left. I grabbed my shoes and purse and ran to the car. When I arrived at the hospital, I found out she was in the intensive care unit. No one seemed to be able to answer my question, "Is she okay?"

As my friends and I sat there wondering what we could do, the nurse came out and said our friend was going to need blood donors. We looked at each other and said, "Let's do it!"

On the drive to the blood bank, we started to get nervous. Everyone was scared to go first, so I volunteered. As the nurse inserted the needle into my arm, I thought, what if everyone would commit an act of kindness for every act of violence committed.

We returned to the hospital, peeking through the window to see our friend. She noticed us and began to smile and wave. We pointed to our arms, showing her that we, too, had wounds, but not as great as hers. Her smile slowly turned to thankful tears.

Although some people say donating blood is no big deal, it was a big deal, not only to me, but also to my friend. It made us stop and think how precious life is and that it *can* happen to you.

--Adrianna Mil

Say It With Flowers

I raise and sell gladiolus flowers. I decided to spare 20 of them for my act of senseless kindness.

I bought packages of Hershey's Kisses and Hershey's Hugs, some tissue paper and ribbon. I wrapped a Kiss and a Hug in the paper and tied them with a ribbon. I typed out 20 messages which read, "You are a special person. Smile." I added the messages to the ribbons and tied them to the gladiolus stems.

I took the flowers to the Rosewood Retirement Center and Health Facility. There, I walked up and down aisles of sick, elderly people and gave them each one of my long-stemmed flowers. I told them I wanted to give them my gift because they are truly special. Some responded with a smile, others with a hug. Many cried. Some told me they didn't think they were special because their children and grandchildren never visited.

I really enjoyed this opportunity to spend some time with these people, give them something and make them feel that there are people in our society who do care about them.

--Stephanie Brannan

Finders Keepers?

During our morning break, two of my friends and I were walking out of our school cafeteria. While we were talking, I saw two sophomore boys bend down to pick up a black wallet. I immediately knew that whatever money that wallet contained, those boys were going to keep it.

Just as I had suspected, they opened the wallet, removed the money and split it on their way to the trash can. I decided I had to do something.

As I approached the boys, they just stared at me. I wasted no time and told them that the wallet belonged to me and that they had to return it at once. I also told them I wanted the money which they had split. They were totally stunned and embarrassed. They gave me the wallet and the money immediately.

I then turned the wallet in to the office and told the secretary the whole story. As I left, two very worried-looking girls came in and asked the secretary if anyone had turned in a black wallet. As she handed the owner her wallet, she told her the story of it's rescue.

Later on, the girl thanked me for returning her wallet and explained how it contained her lunch money for the whole week. I was glad I was able to help. To me, an act of kindness is to help others and to know that I can help make society better.

--Jannette Garcia

A Flower For The Teacher

My friend, Jennifer Waits, and I bought flowers and wrote a card to go with each flower. The cards read, "Just a random act of senseless kindness. Have a good day! From Amelia and Jennifer."

Then we headed to our school and gave a flower to any teacher we could find. The teachers were thrilled to receive flowers from their students.

We had a few flowers left, so we drove around the neighborhood and gave flowers to people getting out of their cars or standing outside their homes. We gave our last flower to a man who didn't want to accept it. We insisted and he said he would pass on the kindness to his wife.

One thing is for sure. Every person Jennifer and I walked away from that afternoon had a wide and beautiful smile on his or her face.

--Amelia Vaca

Good Advice

E ven I, the instigator of the kindness movement, had a little difficulty being kind when I was awakened by a phone call at 2:30 a.m. "Is this the place where I can order a bumper sticker about kindness?" a cheery voiced asked in response to my bleary "hello."

Realizing that I needed to be kind, I brightened up a bit and said, "Of course, it is, but it's 2:30 in the morning and I need a moment to wake up." The woman on the line said she was a night person and forgot about others' sleep habits. I asked from where she was calling and how she found out about the kindness stickers.

While taking a taxi from work to her home in a small community outside of Chicago, she saw the bumper sticker stuck to the back of the front seat of the cab. "In addition, the cab driver had circled your phone number with a note which read: *Everyone should follow this advice!* " she explained.

--Chuck Wall

A "Novel" Idea

Alethea Gasser, a professor in the Humanities Division at Vincennes University, Indiana, came up with a great idea after hearing Chuck Wall speak on the *Hour of Power* television program. She labeled an old animal crackers jar, "RAK," for Random Acts of Kindness. Then she asked the members of her division to write their random acts of kindness on pieces of paper and deposit them in the jar.

Her intent was to solicit the assistance of another professor in reading, sorting, categorizing, adding some art work, and including the accounts in a folder or notebook form. This would then be presented to all members of the division as a Christmas gift at the next year's Christmas party.

What a wonderful way of keeping the spirit of Christmas all year long, Professor Gasser!

...And The Blind Shall See

I volunteered some of my time to the Braille Center at a pancake breakfast fund-raiser. I spent busy hours serving pancakes and talking to people at the breakfast. There was one conversation, in particular, which had a great effect on me.

My conversation was with a gentle, friendly, and tender man. When I first looked at him, I had no idea that he was blind. I wasn't aware of his blindness until he told me about his seeing-eye dog, Sprocket, and how they'd traveled around the country. I saw his great independence and love of life. I felt selfish about how much I take for granted, especially my sight. Blindness did not bother my new friend. "Blindness," he said, "is my special gift from God."

I felt that an act of kindness had been done to me that day. Much of my ignorance about the blind vanished. Blindness always seemed like a tremendous handicap to me. After visiting the Braille Center, I realized that I was the blind one.

--Christina Perez

A Penny Saved

A friend of ours is a coupon clipper extraordinaire. She not only clips the coupons for grocery items but then files them carefully in a box by product category. Recently, she says she has started doing something else with her coupons.

As she walks the grocery store aisles, she places unused coupons on the shelf next to the item for which it's intended. She said, "It gives me a good feeling to know that I might be helping someone else who missed the coupon in the paper."

--Chuck and Di Wall

Pedaling Smiles

There is no written code on the bike trail where I ride in the mornings. All you must do is stay on your side of the path. Some people are doing the family thing, others are exercise buffs and the rest are just out to be out.

People are not usually friendly. It's true that you cannot hold a conversation as you speed by a person on a bike or roller blades, but you can wave. You can say "hi." You can smile and nod your head.

My random act of kindness was nothing big. It was just kind. I waved and smiled at the people on the trail. Kindness starts with baby steps.

--NaheleHoku L. Kaneakalau

For Pete's Sake

A man in upstate New York called me with his story. About 60 years old, Pete is blind and has Parkinson's disease. His mobility is limited as his illness is quite advanced, so he uses a wheelchair. However, he finds time to brighten the lives of others with disabilities via his telephone. People all over upstate New York know about Pete and call on him to talk with a loved one who is having a tough time dealing with a disability. This alone is story enough, but there's more.

Recently, a group in his hometown got bags of groceries together at Christmas to give to those they thought were in need. A very surprised Pete and his wife received four bags the day before Christmas. Now for Pete's act of kindness.

He and his wife contacted a friend who agreed to help them. Pete knew of two families who were really struggling. Pete's friend took the four bags of groceries to the families and presented them as coming from an anonymous friend. Pete knew that no matter how bad things might be for him, there were others in greater need.

--Chuck Wall

Santa's Helpers

C hristmas is a perfect time to commit acts of kindness. Last Christmas, my wife, Di, and I decided to handle gift-giving a little differently. Our middle class family has mastered the "needs" part of our lives. Now we spend more time on the "wants." But this Christmas, rather than giving the usual sweater, perfume, tool, or magazine subscription, we told our family that we wouldn't be giving them traditional gifts. Instead, we joined our friends, John and Donna Hoxsie, in an adventure.

Donna took the leadership role and collected money from us and others and bought stuffed animals. On Christmas Eve, with John dressed as Santa Claus, we went to our county hospital to visit the children's ward. Santa visited each room and let the children each select an animal. We spent time with one 9-year-old boy who had no visitors at all. Visiting with him made the experience worth more than we expected.

We had a few gifts left, so we went to the emergency room. It was filled with the low murmurs and silent crying of adults and children. There, Santa made his rounds with candy and gifts. By the time we left, the room was alive with happy sounds and uplifted voices. What a joyous way to spend Christmas!

--Chuck Wall

Movie Magic

I was waiting in line to see a Sunday movie matinee and I noticed the lady in back of me. She had five kids with her, the youngest probably four and the oldest about 12. She wore old, ripped, cut-off jeans and a stained, white T-shirt. Her kids weren't dressed much better. Clearly, she didn't have much money; but the thought of her taking her kids to the movies impressed me in some way.

I wanted to do something for her, but what? Then it clicked in my head to buy her two tickets. So I bought my ticket then told the woman in the booth that I needed two more tickets for the lady behind me.

I got my ticket and went in with my friends. As I gave my ticket to the usher, I looked back and saw the lady with the five kids smiling.

--Angela Totzke

Give It Up

H ow's this for an idea about kindness? The San Diego Blood Bank created a poster to encourage people to give blood. The slogan, alongside a drawing of a full pint of donated blood reads: "One Random Unit of Senseless Kindness."

--Lynn Sted

O ne day, Katie and I were selling lemonade for 50 cents. The same day, a lady was working so hard, we gave her a free cup and she said, "Thank you very much!" I said, "It was nothing." So, from then on, we sold lemonade for free.

--Danielle, age 8

Nothing Trashy Here

W ilkins Park, near my house, is also known as "gutter park." One afternoon I took a trash bag and spent half an hour picking up most of the trash, beer bottles and cans in the park. When I left the park, it looked much nicer.

It made me feel good to do something to make my neighborhood a little bit nicer. As a student, I am very busy with activities at school, and I often forget about things like my neighborhood. I appreciated the reward of walking around in a clean park and the knowledge that I helped keep it that way for a few days.

--Ernie Minner

Helpless Hummers

There in my hanging creeping Charlie were two fragile hummingbird babies, desperately gasping in the 109-degree heat. I watched with helpless concern as Mother Hummer occasionally flew in and out without adequately attempting to quench the thirst of her offspring.

My friend, John, stopped by to chat. John is tall and strong, brown from years in the construction industry, a beer-drinking, manly man whose language is colorful and direct. He showed great interest in the plight of the hummers, but left after a short while.

Less than an hour later, I peeked out the window to see this brute of a man balanced gracefully on a ladder, gently filling the tiny beaks with sweet, red nectar from my feeder. The wee ones gratefully stretched up to the eye dropper he held with care.

A week later, the pair fluttered their wings and left the creeping Charlie for a healthy hummingbird life.

Thanks, John.

--Sally Hill

A Different Kind of Super Man

My husband, Jim, and I were discussing which store to go to first on our list of things to do. As we were heading toward a busy intersection, Jim was in the far right lane. Suddenly he pulled to the right, stopped quickly, and told me he would be right back as he hopped out of the car.

Because I have no sight, I had no idea of what was going on. In two or three minutes, Jim was back in the car. He explained that he had pulled over to help a man who was trying to push his van to the side of the road. It had stalled in the middle of the intersection. After they got the van to the side, the man yelled a quick "thanks" to Jim, who replied, "No problem."

On another occasion, we were headed to the grocery store and had just turned into the parking lot. The minute we turned in, Jim started laughing. There was a grocery cart picking up speed and heading straight for the most beautiful, new, green BMW. The car was obviously parked in the middle of the lot, straddling a parking line, with no car near it, to save it from dings.

Jim stopped our car and ran out to block the inevitable crash. Laughing the whole way, we knew the owner of the incredible car would never know that his or her pride and joy had been in so much danger. I wonder how often things like this happen of which we're never aware.

--Joan Brock

W hen my dad and I were on vacation and we were trying to get to Okinawa, we couldn't get any seats and my dad's leave was running out. When my dad told me that, these people heard him. They came over and offered to sell us their tickets because they still had a lot of leave left. We thanked them and we got back on time!

--Andy, age 9

An Original Practitioner

M y son and I were visiting the community of Kernville, California, and we were scheduled to ride a raft down the Kern River. We had scheduled this trip with an outfit known as "Outdoor Adventures." On boarding the bus in Kernville, I was quite impressed with the bus driver, David Vance.

Above his driver's seat was printed the phrase, "Practice Random Kindness and Senseless Acts of Beauty." I asked David about it. "When acts of kindness are random and, thereby, unexpected," he said, "they mean more, for they are practiced for the pure enjoyment of the giving."

David was very entertaining and engaging to the bus full of tourists. When he would slow down on the road and pull over for other vehicles, the tourists presumed we were being stopped by the police. David merely pointed to the phrase he had written on the bus. Everyone on board smiled and laughed and waited for the cars to pass. At one point, he even stopped the bus along the side of the road, put on his emergency blinkers, and helped an elderly couple cross a busy section of the road to get to the river. What an original one-of-a-kind person!

--Lynn

Lynn's story ends here but there's more. I spoke with David about this story and also caught up on his life, as coincidentally, he is a former student of mine. He told me that the kindness sign in his bus was a great way to encourage passengers to behave properly. He said that on occasion when people get a bit rowdy, he merely points to the sign which seems to calm them down immediately. I agree with the writer-David is a remarkable person. We all can learn from his attitude toward life.

--Chuck Wall

A Lesson In Kindness

T om Cornford, a teacher in the Fruitvale School District in Bakersfield, California, took on a difficult assignment at summer school. He decided to introduce the concept of kindness to a group of 7-year-old second graders. In the 10-day class, the students performed skits on kindness, made puppets for puppet shows about kindness, watched videos on kindness, and he asked the children and their parents to report on kind things they'd done at home.

The skits the students performed were based on the well-known story, The Good Samaritan, and told the familiar tale of the man who was beaten by thieves, left to die, and was ultimately helped by a Samaritan. Then Cornford put the story into a setting common to children, a school hallway where one child is taunted by bullies. "It was an incredible experience to be part of as I saw each one of the second grade students catch the meaning of kindness in the two stories," Tom said.

The deeds done by the children reflected the lessons from class. The children's parents reported that their children helped get breakfast for younger siblings, emptied dishwashers, took care of the family after a mother had minor surgery, folded laundry, and washed cars.

Tom said his twenty-nine 7-year-olds caught the kindness fever. "I get excited thinking about all that the students would be able to do if kindness were presented to them throughout the entire school year," he said. "This is an exciting and life-changing experience."

One day, my friend and I were walking home together and a puppy started following us. We picked her up and we thought her name should be Magic. I thought, "Maybe I can keep Magic." I did for awhile, but then my dad got home and he said we were going to find the owner. We went door to door asking, "Is this your dog?" All of them said no except for the owner that we found a few minutes later. We were so happy!

--Alex, age 9

The Miracle Worker

A s I sat on the hard bench in the clinic in Nogales, Sonora, Mexico, my head still bleeding from the accident, I remember I was saying, "Doesn't anybody here speak English?" Although I was familiar with Spanish, the trauma of the last hour had left me dazed and unable to think in anything but English. Two of my daughters were seated on my right, uninjured, while my son, on my left, was complaining that his neck hurt. My husband was trying to find out where they had taken our third daughter, who had been covered with a blanket since the "green wagon" had picked us up on the highway south of Nogales.

Now the police had come to arrest my husband since the other driver involved in the auto and truck collision had disappeared. Suddenly there was a woman named Carmen, a bustling, no-nonsense kind of person, listening to my story while rapidly speaking Spanish to the police and waving them away with her hands. Then she turned to the medical personnel behind the reception desk and spoke as if giving instructions. We learned that our third daughter had died before the "wagon" picked us up. The remaining five of us were taken in another wagon (an ambulance?) across the United States-Mexico border to a hospital in Nogales, Arizona.

In the U.S., I was taken to an emergency room where a doctor applied a local anesthetic and stitched up my head wounds. When I awoke several hours later, I was told that my son was diagnosed with a broken neck and was rushed by ambulance to Children's Hospital in Tucson, Arizona. My husband, of course, had gone with him. So, where were my other two little girls? The woman named Carmen had taken them to her home for the night. Who was this Carmen that she could bring about such "miracles" as she had across the border? She was Carmen Leyva from Nogales, Arizona, who was visiting her brother in the Nogales Sonora Clinic, her brother, the Mayor of Nogales.

For the next two days, while I was recovering, Carmen and Miguel Leyva cared for my girls as if they were their own, including them in holiday festivities and bringing them to see me in the hospital. When my sister-in-law arrived to take the girls home, pictures were taken and addresses were exchanged. I was to go to Tucson to be with my son, who, in spite of a broken neck, had no paralysis. There were tears shed when the time came to leave, for in the midst of tragedy, we had found that aura of light known as human kindness.

During the weeks that followed, the Leyvas, with the help of the mayor, were able to find the mortuary where our other little daughter had been taken. Through their efforts, her body was recovered and shipped home to California for burial. We have never seen the Leyvas since that long ago day, although for years we exchanged letters and pictures. Sometimes, I am sad we lost touch, but we will never lose touch with the memory of such kindness shown to strangers with a desperate need!

--Jan Deaton Rockoff

Sometimes We're Pitched a Curve

My mother and I were headed for my baseball game where I was to be starting pitcher. We weren't familiar with the location of the field and it was 15 minutes until game time.

As we were driving, we saw a lady in the middle of the road trying to push her heavy car off to the side and into a parking lot. Her car had run out of gas and no one would stop to help her.

The woman was shocked when I stopped. She said about 100 hundred cars just drove around her. She was really scared because she was alone and in a strange city. It just so happened that I had a gas can in my car and went to a gas station and got gas for her. When I returned, the lady thanked me again and again.

Although I was late to my baseball game and didn't get to pitch until later in the game, I felt like a winner helping that lady.

--M. Brenden Hall

And Have A Nice Day!

I had just heard Chuck Wall speak at the Million Dollar Round Table in Dallas on random acts of kindness when I found myself waiting in line at a drive-up window to order lunch. The line was long and seemed to not be moving very fast. As we finally started to move, a car quickly pulled in line in front of me. I was furious! Then I remembered the random acts of kindness. I tried to think of a better response than screaming obscenities at the man.

So, when I got to the order microphone, I ordered a cookie and asked the clerk to give it to the "gentleman" in front of me. As the interloper reached the drive-through window, I could see him shaking his head and trying to refuse my gift. But the clerk persuaded him that the cookie was paid for and he should just enjoy it.

I felt great the rest of the day.

--Micki Hoesley

Bridging the World With Kindness

My oldest brother, Ty Pritchett, is a linguist for the United States Department of Defense and was attending the Dante Alighieri School in Florence, Italy, a private school that teaches Italian to foreigners. After completing his classes, he took the next 10 days to tour Europe and indulge his favorite hobby, photography.

While photographing the brightly colored houses on the island of Murano, a city similar to Venice with an extensive system of canals, he happened upon a couple of cute kids who were playing on the steps of a house on a canal. As he photographed them, they were happy and glad for the attention.

Three years later, Ty returned to the language school and to Murano for more pictures. He specifically had the same kids in mind, hoping to see if they were there and more grown up. But when he got to Murano, he couldn't remember the exact location. He was carrying photos from the previous trip and wandered for some time hoping to find the neighborhood and asking people if they recognized the children.

Finally, Ty spotted a couple of girls who seemed about the right age and showed them the pictures. One of the girls quickly took off running, with no explanation. She ran up to a house and talked to a woman there, demanding, "Mom, come see!" Ty showed the mother the photographs and she began to cry. One of the photos was a heartwarming depiction of her son who had died in a motorcycle accident a year earlier.

After the death of her son, the mother had gone to all of the neighbors to find any pictures that might exist of her son. There were sadly very few. She thought that she had all of the pictures that she would ever have of the beloved boy. The woman tearfully told Ty that she thought it was a miracle that he would come by with the pictures.

Ty had made copies before he left, in hopes of finding the children. The mother was overwhelmed with gratitude when he presented them to her. She invited Ty to be an honored guest in their home where he was treated "like a visiting president." He shared a fish dinner and their best bottle of wine. Images of Italy will be forever in Ty's thoughts.

--Janet Crosby

The Wisdom of Solomon from Another King

I n 1967, while working for KRON-TV Channel 4 in San Francisco, Dr. Martin Luther King, Jr. came into the studio one Sunday morning to be the guest on *Meet the Press*. I don't remember if the following story was told during his interview or after, when I spoke with him, but I have never forgotten his message. I believe it sums up some of our reluctant willingness to help each other in times of need.

"Imagine yourself walking down a dark street in the center of town. As you are beginning to cross an alley, you notice that a man is walking alone on the other side of the same street and is also stepping across the alley. As you glance across the street, another man rushes out of the alley and begins beating the other pedestrian. The man being attacked begins to shout for help.

"What goes immediately through your mind is something like this. 'If I go over and help that man, what's going to happen to me?' What we should be saying to ourselves is, 'If I don't go over and help that man, what's going to happen to him?' We are so concerned about ourselves that we will ignore the welfare of others by thinking first of our own concerns."

-- Dr. King

Yes, we must be concerned with our own safety, but I believe what Dr. King is pointing out with his story is the fact that we have become a "me" society where we seem little concerned with our fellow man unless there is something in it for us personally. As our Kindness song says, "We need to stop thinking of the me, me, me, and begin thinking of the YOU, YOU, YOU."

--Chuck Wall

It's Raining Kindness

O ne afternoon as my friend and I were leaving the bank, it started to rain. We ran for the car before we got totally soaked. Parked next to us was a car with the trunk open and an elderly lady struggling with an umbrella and groceries.

I approached her and caught her by surprise. "Excuse me, may I help you with your groceries?" I asked. She said, "I would really appreciate it. I'm not as young as I used to be. The wind is really strong today, and it's all I can do to hold onto my umbrella."

My friend and I put the groceries into the trunk of her car. We held her umbrella until she was in the driver's seat, folded the umbrella and handed it to her. She thanked us and said how refreshing it was to find someone who would help out a total stranger.

--Shannon Nicole Carter

Food for the Soul

T here is a bridge near my home. Many homeless people live underneath it. Many look hungry and scared. I decided I would take one of them a plate of food. I knew it wasn't much, but maybe it would help.

My mother made dinner. She cooked fried chicken, mashed potatoes, green beans, and made fruit salad. I took my plate and covered it with foil. Then I got into my car and drove to the bridge. I figured that these people miss many meals, so one wouldn't hurt me.

When I got to the bridge, I saw many homeless people. I wanted to be able to feed them all. I glanced to my right and saw an entire family. The kids were so skinny. They were the only ones who saw that I had food. I knew I just couldn't walk past them and give the food to someone else, so I approached them and gave them my plate. I told them I was going to go home and get more food.

Fortunately, my mom had some food left over. I told her what happened and we made three small plates of food. We even found a bag of clothes sitting in the garage waiting for our next garage sale. My mom and I took the food and clothes back to the family. They were so grateful.

I cannot describe the feeling I had inside. Knowing that I touched the lives of people made me feel so good about myself. I wanted to go home and make dinner for all the homeless people in the world. I realize that I cannot be responsible for all the starving people in the world, but if everyone made a conscious effort, the world would be a much happier place.

--Angela Cook

One day, my friend fell off his bike and he was bleeding. I didn't have a Band-Aid, but I had a handkerchief and I wrapped it around his leg until he got a Band-Aid. I also let him keep the handkerchief and he said, "Thank you." He said if it happens to me, he would have a Band-Aid. This is a random act of kindness.

--Chrysanta, age 9

A Crushed Crusader

M ark Hyman, producer of *The Crusaders* television show, decided to carry out an act of kindness on the Bronx Whitestone Bridge. He walked up to the toll plaza and gave the toll operator enough money to pay for the next 12 cars crossing the bridge. The toll operator told Mark that in his 30 years on the toll bridge, he had never had anyone offer to pay for someone else's toll.

Mark knew he had an idea that would touch the hearts of at least 12 people. He wanted a record of their reactions, so he positioned himself and a video crew at the side of the road with a clear view of the drivers' faces.

As his crew was beginning to video tape the first driver's expression, they heard sirens in the distance. They got closer and closer. In a matter of moments, two New York City Police cars skidded to a stop in front of them. The police piled out of the cars and promptly arrested Mark for "filming on a bridge without a permit."

Some people just don't get it!

The Kindness of Strangers

H ere's a letter that appeared in the July 20, 1996, edition of The Bakersfield Californian newspaper.

Recently my four children and I stopped for lunch at a local coffee shop. Because there are so many of us, normally we opt for the drive-through type of fare. But on that day, we decided to test our restaurant manners.

We were seated in a booth in the corner that forces you to be a part of someone else's lunch - whether they like it or not. A woman was already seated there with her newspaper - I think anticipating a quiet time with her lunch and reading.

This situation can be particularly terrifying for anyone sitting down to lunch with four children, two of them ready for naps. We settled down and had a brief conversation about our concern about the bill and what we should order. We managed to order plenty and still have enough to spare for a tip.

After eating, and fairly good behavior on everyone's part, we waited patiently for the check. Finally, we went up to ask for our bill. What we found to our surprise was the woman sitting near us had not only tolerated us as lunch companions, but paid for our bill, without a word, asking the waitress to say nothing.

She left without a thank you and she left us with a very nice feeling that we're all determined to pass along. We wish we could have thanked her. We thought since she was reading the paper that day that, hopefully, she will again today.

--Carrie Fanucchi

One day when I brought my lunch to school, I saw a girl named Kristina who said she didn't have a lunch or lunch money. Before I knew it, I had asked her if she wanted to share my lunch. She said that was very nice of me and that she appreciated it.

--Audra, age 8

It's Contagious!

I have always thought of myself as a positive, confident person, but something was missing. I was satisfied that I helped others, but it was on my terms and in accordance with my timeline. Even today, I still volunteer my time and give money to causes I believe in, but those are planned, organized efforts.

I took the kindness message to heart and tried out the concept of randomly giving kindness to others - family, friends, work-mates, even strangers. You know what? The void was filled with happiness. Most of the cracks in the seams of the puzzle that is me were solidified and strengthened. I knew I was having an impact on the world, because random acts of kindness are contagious. Those who receive find ways to release that positive feeling to someone else, who in turn releases it to someone else. At times, it grows exponentially.

Random acts of kindness don't take much time or energy and virtually no planning. Just give kindness when someone is in need. You will have caught the fever and you will know you are having an impact. But remember, you must practice, practice, practice.

--Charlette Sears

Don't Shelf This Act

My neighbor said she wished her husband had time to put up a shelf in her daughter's room for the child's dolls. I have all the woodworking tools needed to make a nice shelf with decorative edges, as well as brackets.

I went to the lumber store and chose a good piece of pine shelving. I used my router to finish the edges and sanded it smooth. I used my scroll saw to cut out some fancy brackets and finished the edges on them as well.

When I presented my neighbor with the shelf and brackets, she was delighted. She said it was perfect and more than she had imagined for the room. It was a simple thing for me to make the shelf and brackets, but it meant so much to her.

--Byron Jespersen

Pumped Up With Kindness

My car was running low on gas on a blistering hot day, so I stopped to fill it up. I reached a gas station and pulled right up to the only available pump. By the time I got out of my car and gave the merchant my credit card, another car had pulled up directly behind me at the pump.

I noticed an elderly couple inside the car looking slightly agitated. They were watching my every move. The other lanes of the station were full with waiting cars, also. I looked over at the elderly couple waiting behind me and signaled for them to move up and take my spot as I moved out of the way. It was hot and I sensed that they needed to get on their way. As it turns out, they did. They were en route to the medical center to see a grandchild who was gravely ill.

They noticed my "kindness" bumper sticker and thanked me for making them my random act for the day. I moved in a couple of cars behind them, bought them some water bottles, and gave them a bumper sticker (I carry extra in my car). Their faces lit up briefly and I felt as if some of their hope had been restored.

--Diane Oglesby

Carried By Love

This story by Gretchen Penner, daughter of Dr. Robert Schuller, has appeared in print before, but, with her permission, I felt it should be told again.

--Chuck Wall

It was 4:30 a.m. when I was awakened by the ringing phone. I heard my mother's voice on the other end of the line. "Gretchen, Dad's in emergency brain surgery right now in Amsterdam. We need to pray for him." My heart sank. This was it, the call I had always dreaded.

"What happened?" I asked. "We don't know," Mom replied as she went into the details of how Dad was found collapsed in his room. With a deep breath and a shaky voice I asked, "What are his chances?" fearful of the answer. "If they can find where the bleeding is coming from, then they will be pretty good," Mom said.

"If" and "pretty good." Not much of an answer. In other words, we did not know, but at that point, it did not sound too promising. I turned to Jim, my husband, and he held me tight as I cried, and he prayed.

The first person I called was a board member of the church and a dear friend, Richard Watts, who recently lost his father to cancer. Knowing that he would understand the fear and pain I was experiencing, I woke him up with the news and, within half an hour, Richard was at our house talking with us, praying with us, and supporting us.

It so happened that a girlfriend was visiting from out of town that weekend. God could not have planned it better. When I told her the situation, she offered to do whatever she could to help. At my request, Holly helped baby-sit my baby. Knowing that my daughter was in good hands, I felt free to go help my mother.

By the time I got to the house, my brother, Bob, was already there, greeting me with a hug. As I sat down to talk with Bob and Mom, I could hardly believe how strong my mother was. She had the strength of an eagle, and she had a peace like a dove. Even though she knew the possibility that Dad might not make it home alive, she said, "I have released him to God. He's in God's hands."

It was not long before more family and friends started gathering at the house. At 8:30 a.m. we began waiting with anticipation for each phone call update from Amsterdam. During those long hours, both my biological and spiritual family were all joined in thoughts and prayers. By 1 p.m., the prayers were answered as we finally knew that Dad would be okay.

On the day of the accident, church-family members delivered muffins and brought food for lunch. Some stayed and sat quietly with us as each phone call came. Others gave a quick hug and show of support, then left. And still others stayed at home in uninterrupted prayer, or went to the church to lift their prayers. Throughout the week as I struggled, waiting for my father to return home and then have a second surgery, the prayers and love kept flowing in. I received phone calls, hugs and flowers. Never before had I felt so much strength coming from outside forces.

Christ and the church--not the building, but the people--was the strength I needed. That is why I praise this church so highly. The Crystal Cathedral is a church that cares! It's people who love and care for each other, who are willing to do anything they can to help. God worked through those around me to carry me over that rough road.

Many know the story entitled "Footprints" in which the man looks back and sees one set of footprints on the sand during a difficult time in his life and asks, "God, where were you?" God replies, "There, next to you. Those are not your footprints you see but mine, for I was carrying you." Well, when I look back at that day and week of my father's accident, I don't see one set of footprints, I see hundreds, and not one of them belong to me.

--Gretchen Penner

People With Real Heart

At Coastal Cardiology Consultants in Palm Harbor, Florida, they do more than just mend hearts. Helen M. Erickson wrote and asked if I minded that she took my kindness slogan and wrote it on the food donation box they keep in the office's kitchen.

The office has "adopted" a family in need for an entire year. The family is a single mother with three small children who was abused by her spouse and then abandoned.

"Mainly we help out with food and clothes and Christmas gifts during the holidays and food all year round," Helen wrote. "It's a wonderful feeling to help someone else and I am so proud of my co-workers who are responding to this family in such a generous way."

A New Approach
By The Pepsi Generation

A cold Pepsi can really hit the spot, especially when it's 102 degrees! For my act of kindness, I bought a 12-pack of Pepsi, put it on ice in a cooler, and headed for the river.

The park was more crowded than I had ever seen it. At first I was almost intimidated, so I decided to get into the water and act natural. After 30 minutes, I grew thirsty. I got out of the water and walked along the shore.

I decided to give a soda to a young boy first. He was scared, shook his head and ran. I was crushed. A bigger boy, who looked like the other one's brother, walked up to me and smiled. I held up a Pepsi. He nodded, took it, smiled and skipped away.

Some people were skeptical and some were very trusting. They all took a soda, gave me warm smiles, and I was happy. I believe this was a sincere, kind act, and I believe my quenched, satisfied feeling proves that.

--Lucas Rucks

Hakuna Matata

M y friend Nancy is a recent graduate of Stockdale High School and the mother of two-year-old Rosita. Nancy and her family struggle financially. While Nancy is working or attending college, her daughter is with a baby-sitter. So I decided to help out by treating Rosita to a special day out.

I picked Rosita up from the sitter at 2:30 p.m. and we went to McDonald's. Rosita was delighted to find a bag of goodies waiting on the front seat. What really affected me was her concern about sharing all of her new found treasures with her little friend, Lily.

I put her new Lion King dress and sandals on her in the car just before we went in to eat. When we entered McDonald's, Rosita insisted on sitting on the giant Ronald McDonald. She ate her Happy Meal on it, also. When she finished, I took her to the playground outside. It really made me smile to hear the sound of her high-pitched giggles. When she had her fill of fun, we headed back home.

Rosita is lucky to have a mom like Nancy who teaches her and nurtures her. Nancy was very appreciative of what I did, although, I'm not quite sure that it benefited little Rosita as much as it benefited me.

--Rosie Loya

'Tis The Season

We discovered that our friend and co-worker, Vernie, was having a particularly hard time financially. Her ex-husband had been in a car wreck and his medical bills and inability to return to work left everyone extremely short on extra income. Vernie had no money to buy Christmas presents for her red-haired, blue-eyed, 12-year-old daughter. We decided we couldn't let Vernie feel as though she had let her daughter down at a most important time in a child's life.

We purchased several gifts and then "borrowed" Vernie's car keys on Christmas Eve when she was away from her desk. We loaded the gifts onto the back seat of her car, then replaced her keys.

We all waited as Vernie left. She stood next to her car in tears and amazement. We all shared her tears of happiness as we watched through the second-story windows at the parking lot below.

--Cindy Landry

A Routine Visit

Dianna, who had been looking for something she might do to demonstrate her compassion and interest in the community, came up with a simple idea that not only she could experience, but also her 8-year-old daughter. She called a local convalescent hospital to inquire about visiting patients during regular visiting hours. The warm voice on the other end of the line assured Dianna that a visit would be most welcomed and appreciated by her relatives staying in the hospital. When Dianna explained she had no relatives or friends there, the initial response was silence.

Eventually, the warm voice said, "Well, if you just want to visit, I guess that's all right. When would you like to visit?" Dianna responded she would come on Tuesday afternoon and asked if it was okay to bring her daughter. She had never been to a convalescent hospital and Dianna felt she would benefit from the experience. It was fine with the hospital staff.

On Tuesday, Dianna and her daughter presented themselves at the reception desk and explained their mission. "We just want to say hello to those staying here and, perhaps, learn a little about their lives. Maybe we can offer a little encouragement and let them know we care about them." With that, mother and daughter began walking halls, entering rooms, and merely offering a smile and friendly conversation.

Later Dianna said, "You know, I don't know who benefited more from this experience, the patients in the hospital or my daughter and me, but it doesn't make much difference now. Because for quality time, my daughter and I visit hospitals regularly because we know our visits are really appreciated by those recovering from surgery or illness. And it has brought my daughter and I closer together. I think other parents might try this as a way of bringing cheer into some lives and closeness into their own family relationships."

The Kindest Memories

T wo random acts of kindness happened to me many years ago, but I still remember it. I was a new bride and had gone to the store to get some groceries. I was very aware that I didn't have much money in my purse because it was the day before my husband's payday and we were broke as usual.

I was trying to add up the running cost of the items I was putting on the counter, so I would have enough money to pay for them. But when the grocer added up the total, it was 96 cents more than I had.

Embarrassed and unsure of myself, I scratched around in my purse and pockets in the vain hope I could find some loose change. Finally, I realized I would have to put some items back. As I was fumbling around trying to figure out what to remove, an elderly lady standing next to me at the counter said to me, "You probably need those things. Here, take this dollar bill. I have extra money today."

I tried to thank her and get her name and address so I could return the money, but she just said, "No, pass it along some day when you find someone in a fix like yours."

I'll never forget her kindness and I have passed it along...

Some years ago, I got on a bus in Cleveland, Ohio, to go to the Western Reserve University Library. At that time, the bus fare was 25 cents.

I paid my fare and took a vacant seat right next to the bus driver. When the bus came to the next stop, a rather scruffy-looking young lady got on, looked a bit shame-faced and told the driver she didn't have any money for the fare. Thinking she was probably a student, I had a quarter in my pocket and stood up and dropped it in the fare box.

In the meantime, she had asked the bus driver where the bus was going. He told her and she said, "Oh, this isn't the bus I want," and got off. The bus driver looked back at me, grinned, and said, "I doubt if she knows where she wants to go, but if I have another customer who can't pay the fare, I'll let him or her ride on your quarter."

--Doris Redies

Watch the Birdie!

In 25 years of bird watching, my husband and I have only seen the little Green Kingfisher once. It is the smallest of our kingfishers and is a common resident along the lower Rio Grande Valley in Texas.

We took a three-week "birding" trip, following the Rio Grande from Presidio, Texas, down to the lower Rio Grande Valley. We saw 136 species of birds, but no Green Kingfisher. As we wandered the back roads of Texas, heading back towards California, we drove through the small town of Refugio. Suddenly, I grabbed my husband's arm and screamed, "Stop!"

There on a signboard in front of the Chamber of Commerce building was the message: GREEN KINGFISHER WAS SEEN IN CITY PARK. We located the park, wandered along the small river and zoom! Right past our eyes flew a beautiful male Green Kingfisher. He was feeding up and down the river, but stayed in the area where he and a mate were nesting. He perched right in front of us several times, allowing us to fill our binoculars and memories with his beauty.

After returning to Bakersfield, I wrote a letter of thanks to the Refugio Chamber of Commerce for putting up the sign for transient "birders" passing through. I also commented that it was too bad that their beautiful little river was cluttered with paper litter, cans, bottles, rusted metal and discarded tires.

The Refugio newspaper, <u>Advantage Press</u>, printed my letter and sent me a copy. About a month later, the Chamber of Commerce sent me a letter and another copy of the <u>Advantage Press</u> showing pictures of local birders and friends cleaning up the river. One picture showed a man hauling out a load of 25 tires.

What a great, double benefit. Their act of kindness letting us know the Green Kingfisher was there made our trip special. And my letter obviously motivated the people of Refugio to clean up their pretty river.

--Shirley Rodewald

Planting a Little Kindness

My grandparent's next door neighbor has multiple sclerosis. She and my grandmother started chatting about gardens one day while I was visiting. The woman mentioned she would love pretty flowers like my grandmother's.

Just by chance, my mother had bought a few flowers but had not planted them. She said I could have them after I told her what I wanted to do.

I went to the woman's house the next day and told her that she didn't have to ask any longer because I was going to do it for her. I showed her the flowers and my tools when she thought I was joking. She couldn't believe it!

The woman was very thankful afterwards and offered to pay me, but I told her that wasn't necessary.

"God is watching you, and one day He will reward you," she told me as I was cleaning up. That made me feel better than any amount of money she could have given me.

--Leigh-Ann Smart

Take A Tip

I was in the parking lot at PayLess Drug Store. A man on crutches and his young daughter came out of the store. The little girl could barely reach the handle of the cart she was pushing, but her happy expression indicated her contentment in just being with her father. As they headed for the parking lot, the child pushed the cart over the curb. The cart tipped over and everyone around turned to see what happened.

They all watched as the young girl and her father tried to turn the cart upright again. Another man and I rushed forward to help them. The man on crutches was tired from the struggle and very thankful for the help. As he and his daughter walked away, he thanked us once again.

At first I felt good, but later I began to wonder what would have happened if neither the other man nor I hadn't been around when the cart tipped over. Random acts of senseless kindness need to be carried out even more, so that the next time not just two people but four, five, or six come to help.

--Eddie Ganzinotti

Renewed By Reading

I volunteered to read every day for an hour or so to a woman who has multiple sclerosis which has paralyzed her. Before she was unable to hold a book in her hands, she was a voracious reader.

At first I was nervous. I didn't know this woman, and I had never read out loud to someone before. I was afraid that I would sound bland and boring. But the lady didn't make fun of me. Instead, she helped me with the hard-to-pronounce words. It made me feel better about myself.

While I was at her home, we would also sit and talk. We talked about anything that was on our minds, and she even gave me advice about something that was bothering me. She told me that she appreciated me coming to read and that it made her day.

As I went to the lady's house throughout the week, I felt more and more comfortable. It actually became fun to read to her. I felt as if I had accomplished something great!

--Brenda Phillips

A Kindness for a Kindness

When Jeff Berlent of <u>The Herald Baldwin</u> newspaper in Long Beach, New York, called me for an interview, I'm sure it was just another assignment for him. However, as we all know, life takes us in directions which we do not always plan. Here is Jeff's story.

I was driving on the Wantagh Expressway when my car suddenly spun out of control. As my car was spinning, as well as my life before my eyes, many things crossed by mind. Along with the usual types of thoughts like those of accomplishments yet to be achieved and hope that my car would not flip over, one thought was of a 90-year old gentleman who came into our office, "...because (he) had no friends and just needed to talk to someone."

My car did land in a safe place and, although I was shaken, I was not seriously hurt. I then saw your words in action. Two cars stopped and a man and a woman came to rescue me. They asked if I needed help. I said, "Yes, thank you for providing it for me."

I know I could have just sent a copy of the paper, but I wanted you to know that our conversation was not just another article. It provided me with insights into a more pleasant reality.

Lights Out!

I pulled into the parking lot at California State University, Bakersfield, and parked next to a Honda Civic. I noticed the headlights were still on after the morning commute. I saw the car doors were unlocked, so I proceeded to turn off the lights. I started to walk away when I noticed a young man frantically running out of a nearby building, waving his arms wildly. He thanked me profusely and really appreciated that I had taken the trouble to watch out for someone else.

--Carolyn Stover

Taking Kindness Into Account(ing)

As I sat behind Mary in class, I could see that she was struggling to grasp the concept of accounting. After several class periods, I could hear doubt and defeat in her words. I wanted to help so I gave her my phone number and offered to assist in any way I could.

During the next two weeks, I saw Mary continue to struggle and asked why she hadn't called. She replied that she had not wanted to trouble me. I reassured her that I wouldn't have given her my number if I had not meant for her to use it.

Mary did start calling shortly thereafter, and we were able to work through the difficulties she had been having. Through this simple act of kindness, a friendship blossomed. Perhaps, this was the greatest reward.

--Karina K. Crosby

Simplicity

W hen I was at the grocery store last week, I noticed that there weren't any shopping carts left inside the store. I was kind of ticked off that I had to search the parking lot for one.

I found a cart, then I noticed a little old lady hobbling into the store. She had trouble walking and getting up onto the curb. I gave her my cart. She accepted with a smile. It wasn't a profound act, but it made her day a bit easier.

I feel silly writing about this experience. Acts of kindness shouldn't be broadcast and boasted about. They should be everyday occurrences, genuine and sincere.

--Amy Gillick

The Fare Deal

My friend, David Peters, and I came up with a plan to pay for the next five people getting on the bus. We wanted to be able to observe the reactions of the individuals affected.

The first three people boarded the bus together and were surprised and smiled when the driver explained their fares had been paid. The driver seemed annoyed at the idea at first, but now he was getting into it.

At another stop, an elderly woman had no reaction to the deed; her face did not break expression. The most complicated situation arose when an elderly Hispanic man boarded the bus.

He was either hard of hearing or spoke no English, because the driver pleaded with him not to pay, but he didn't seem to understand. I admired the driver's determination. After several minutes, the man paid just so the driver could get him to sit down.

There was one more paid fare and at the next stop a man got on and simply exclaimed, "Oh, thanks!" His smile was just as satisfying as the first group's was. I now understand why the (kindness) concept has exploded like it has. If everyone tried to do something, no matter how simple, to help another, this world would be a lot more optimistic.

--Chad Troller

Pride Cometh Before The Fall

I met Opal Young when I was walking my dog. I was always amazed at how well she kept her yard and rose garden, even though she is well into her 70's.

Recently, a neighbor told me Opal had tripped on her porch and broke her foot. I decided to go by and see how she was. When I was walking up to her house, I noticed the yard, in which she took great pride, was overgrown with weeds and fallen leaves.

I rang Opal's doorbell. She came to the door on crutches, obviously with great effort. I asked if she would mind if I came over on Saturday to clean up her yard because I knew she kept it immaculate. She was surprised at my offer.

On Saturday, I went to her house and spent the whole day raking and bagging leaves and weeding her flower beds. She sat on her porch and told me about herself. It struck me then that I would turn this random act of senseless kindness into an ongoing expression of kindness.

I know what I did for Opal made a difference, not only in her life, but in mine, also. It is a shame that more people don't realize that just because someone doesn't ask for help, doesn't mean he or she doesn't need it. By doing something nice for someone, you can make yourself feel needed and appreciated, too.

--Debra Hinkle

Everybody Needs Somebody Sometime

I understand the purity of true, selfless kindness, having experienced it at a time in my life in which I thought I wouldn't need anyone. I learned the poignant truth that we will all need someone sometime.

I had put myself through college without a scholarship, grant or financial help from my parents and was, at last, in the final year of my studies. I had done well for myself, despite the fact that I basically lived in poverty. But the end was near and I was feeling quite proud of myself and my independence. I refer to it as my "Mary Tyler Moore period." You know, "You're going to make it after all."

Then one morning, around 4 a.m., my reality came crashing in - literally. The door was crashed open by a repeat sex offender who had skipped bail in another state. I found it hard to believe that someone wanted to kill me if I didn't cooperate. So that's what I did. Rape proved the lesser evil than death. It is a decision I have lived to never regret.

Looking back, I amaze myself how well I held myself together as I went through agonizing minutes of his crimes. Then finally, to *his* surprise, not mine (*I* was aware of the presence of the police as they rolled in, motors cut, surrounding the house), they kicked the door in, guns pulled. He leapt away from me. They caught him as he tried to run for it out the back of my house.

As impossible as this all seemed, it forced me to see an obvious lesson. I needed my neighbor next door to hear my cries and act correctly and call the police. I needed the police to comprehend the situation correctly and surround the house and catch the man and jail him. I needed the district attorney to represent my case and unequivocally win his argument that this man should be jailed. But, what I didn't know at the time, was that I needed an advocate.

I was lucky enough to be appointed one as the courts deemed necessary for all victims of violent crime. What I learned from her was what true kindness is. It wasn't a duty and it wasn't motivated by my cries for help. It was simply a presence, quietly guiding me back to the trust that sometimes strangers will bestow to a broken spirit.

I am embarrassed to say now, 15 years later, that I don't remember her name. I can picture her face, soft and unquestioning, and yet somehow knowing just what I needed. She didn't offer any advice or even words of encouragement. It was only her presence that I needed.

I felt brave and vulnerable at the same time as I spoke my piece on the stand. When I finished, she told me I had done well and handed me a little box. When I got home and opened the gift, it was an ornate pencil sharpener. It was shaped like an egg, with hand-painted goldfish swimming among thin sea grass. It was simple and functional for a college student. It probably didn't cost very much, but it's smooth surface and size felt reassuring in the palm of my hand.

Now as I hold the egg, I think of this woman and wish I could be more like her. She fleetingly touched my life, much like goldfish must swim in a pond, not with any predetermined course, just knowing that where they are is where they should be at that moment. It is a little prayer I say now to myself that I may be that, too.

--Anne

Dignitary of Kindness

D ixie Van Dyke, switchboard operator at Bakersfield College, shared this story. As she began, she said, "I hope I can make it through without crying. It took place several days ago, but I still feel so good that I start crying every time I think about it."

While standing in line at the grocery checkout counter, I listened to the lady in front of me as she told the clerk, "Would you please put my groceries in plastic bags? My apartment is two blocks away and I need the handles on the plastic bags."

Without really thinking about what I was about to do, but only thinking of your random acts of kindness project, I took two steps forward and said to this stranger, "My car is right out front and I would be glad to give you a ride to your apartment."

The woman protested she couldn't put me to so much trouble, but I persisted and she finally agreed to accept my offer after many "thank-yous" and "you really don't have to do thats."

In the few minutes we had in the car together, I found out she had just moved here from the eastern United States and she knew virtually no one in Bakersfield. She then said something that made this such a special experience for me. "You know, I am 64 years old and this is the first time anyone has ever offered to give me a ride home from the grocery store.

I think I'm going to like living here. For me, you are Bakersfield's Ambassador of Goodwill. God bless you for your kindness."

Once when I was in third grade, I was eating in the cafeteria. My friend, Travis Powers, was very thirsty. He asked me if he could have my drink. I said, "Yes." Anyway, I wasn't that thirsty.

--Dylan, age 9

A Good Bargain

I went to the store for my mom to pick up a couple of items we needed for dinner. I was in the check out line, and the elderly lady in front of me came up about $4 short on her purchase. She was trying to decide what she was going to put back, when I handed the clerk $4 dollars.

Both the clerk and the lady were shocked, and so was my fiancee and friend. My friends have always considered me to be cheap, so it must have been a big surprise to them. It was even a little bit of a surprise to me.

After the shock wore off, the elderly lady thanked me and told me she felt it would be better if there were more young people in the world like me. It was a real learning experience for me and maybe even my friends, who were there to witness this random act of kindness.

--Robert Talley

A Smile From Head to Toe

A s I was cleaning out my closet, I realized I had more shoes than room for them. I decided to give the shoes I didn't wear to someone who wanted them, but who?

One of my little sister's friends was at our house and asked me what I was going to do with all the shoes. I asked her if she would like them. "Of course, if you give them to me," she replied. She tried them on and the shoes fit perfectly. When I told her to take them all, she asked me why I didn't want the shoes. I told her I didn't like them and she said, "Why, if they are brand new?" I realized then that I take a lot of things for granted.

When I saw the little girl again, she was wearing a pair of the shoes that I had given her. I couldn't believe that a pair of my shoes could bring a smile to a little girl's face. Something that can make a person smile is worth more than money can buy.

--Yolanda Mesa

Tour of Duty

In 1967, my husband, George, went to Viet Nam. I stayed behind in San Clemente where many other Marine wives also waited for their husbands to come home. My daughter, Kristin, was just 3 months old when he left, and during the next 13 months, the two of us spent many hours with Marine Corps friends. Military wives, especially those with children, can form a pretty close-knit community and San Clemente was no exception. In that kind of situation many kindnesses are done, but one stands out in my mind as very special.

As the time for George to come home drew near, I learned that I would not know the actual date until he arrived at the air base in Northern California, and that his call would come just minutes before boarding a plane that would bring him to Los Angeles International Airport. I realized it would take me about as much time to drive to the airport as it would take for him to fly there. I had my worries about how I would cope with the drive, the traffic, the baby, and whether I would remember, or have the time, to do everything I wanted to do in our apartment to make it perfect for his homecoming.

It was then that another wife came to visit and said she had been thinking of something she would like to do for me. The moment George called, day or night, I was to call her. She would come over, make sure dishes were done, toys put away, bathroom clean, beds changed, and baby bathed while I went to the airport.

That is exactly what she did.

--Sandra Larson

One time in third grade, we were at our Fab Friday recess. There was a little boy that was lost, so I asked my teacher if I could take him to the office. I took him to the office and he saw his mom. His mom said, "Thank you." It was my way of doing a kindness.

--Jenny, age 8

Kindness, Brother!

Our 55 years of marriage have been dedicated to making the world a better place. We have been involved with many groups as our children were growing up, but our work with random acts of kindness, or RAK, has been the most readily accepted teaching we have ever shared.

For three years, we have worked with teachers in our school district, business organizations, and just anyone who crossed our path, from the mailman to the garbage man, from waitresses to people in doctor's and dentist's waiting rooms.

We travel in our old '78 van and stay in campgrounds. We take hikes and walk on the beach wearing our RAK buttons. When people ask about our buttons, we share information and take their names and addresses to follow-up with more material.

We have met people in all types of work and from all over the country as well as England and Japan. When we stop at gas stations, we offer material to those who see our bumper sticker and want to become involved. We're like a couple of old hippies dealing kindness out of the side of our van instead of drugs.

--Emmetta Allen

Boxes Full of Kindness

When I first set out to commit a random act of senseless kindness, I considered taking lunch to some homeless people. However, after more thought, I decided to do something that would be of benefit for a longer period of time than lunch.

The best way my friend, Dennise, and I could help would be to provide some items that would be of use to others. Each of us searched our homes for clothing and books that we no longer needed. Our next step was to purchase travel-size toothbrushes, toothpaste, Band-Aids, baby items, lotion, shampoo, and conditioner.

Then we took the boxes of items to the homeless shelter to be distributed as the employees saw fit. I noticed many surprised faces as we lifted the boxes out of the car. They were shocked that we were not from an organization, but were helping on our own.

A heart-warming feeling came over me as my friend and I unloaded the many boxes. I really felt that we were doing something that would make a difference in our community. I like to think that we were not only providing needed items, but hope as well.

--Julie Kudchadker

Here, Kitty, Kitty

Every single day was so hard. I ate whatever I could find or catch, but on many days, there was nothing. Sometimes I got injured in fights and the wounds wouldn't heal quickly. My fur was always matted and full of burrs. But worst of all were the winter nights - so long, so cold, and so lonely.

Then I met a spunky little gray cat, a male like me. He seemed pretty nice. I am quite large and most cats his size keep their distance. He just wanted to play and have a good time.

One day, the small cat motioned for me to follow him. We were soon at the mouth of a dark cave. I wasn't going in, but day after day he led me to the cave entrance. Finally, curiosity got the better of me and I peeked in. It was unlike any cave I had ever seen. It was very large, well-lighted, and had no dirt or rocks or mud. I ventured in a few feet and went in a little further each day for a week.

At last, I saw what this was all about. Before me was food, sweet-smelling food fit for a king. After no more than one blissful nibble, however, there they were, the humans! I knew from an encounter earlier in my life that humans were bad. I was out of there in a flash!

At the small cat's urging, I continued to return to sneak some food each day. The humans, though, still spotted me. To my surprise, they always spoke gently and never chased me. Deciding they were only a minor threat, I began lingering long enough to eat my fill.

As the months have gone by, everything has changed so much. Believe it or not, the humans have become one of my favorite pastimes. They brush all the dirt and burrs out of my fur and rub my head. That feels so wonderful. They call me Blue and my friend, Tigger. As far as I'm concerned, Tigger is now my brother, and there was never a better one. I will never forget his act of kindness when I needed it so much.

--Greg and Patsy Randall (Blue's humans)

Taking the Plunge

I t was 6:20 a.m., and I was swimming laps in my daily exercise class. I noticed a man bobbing up and down in the water. Panting from exhaustion, I heard him tell the lifeguard that his keys had come out of the pocket of his swim trunks and were lost in the pool. The lifeguard did nothing to help him, but said, "Good luck finding your keys; the pool is 12 feet deep."

I realized the man had a problem staying under water for more than a few seconds. I swam over to him and asked where he was when he lost his keys. It was somewhere in the deep end, he replied.

The water was so cloudy that I couldn't see a thing. I tightened my goggles, plunged deep under the water, felt around the bottom of the pool for a few seconds, then came up for a breath. I continued searching for at least 20 minutes, all the time feeling a stinging sensation in my ears from the water pressure.

Finally my fingers touched the keys. I was so happy coming up out of the water, I yelled, "I found them!" The man would not stop thanking me. Even though my ears hurt, I felt great inside. My joy came purely from helping that man and the challenge of finding those keys. Acts of kindness are rewarding for the person receiving the kindness, but there is an even greater reward in the experience for the giver.

--Eileen Munoz

A Dream Come True and Remembered

F or many years, my wife, Star, wanted to visit Niagara Falls. So, in the summer of 1996, along with my grandson, Paul, we piled into our motor home for our coast-to-coast escapade.

We pulled into a KOA campground in Lewistown, New York, and the following afternoon, embarked on the long anticipated tour of Niagara Falls. Along on the tour were campground "neighbors" of ours, Don and Jerrie Engel of Merrillville, Indiana. It wasn't until we returned home six weeks later that we learned what special people this vivacious couple are.

In our mail were six photos of us, our tour, surrounding sights, and Don and Jerrie. (They must have gotten our address from the tour people as we hadn't exchanged that information.) Jerrie had been busy on the tour taking pictures and capturing memories. On each of the photographs she had written dates and comments. As we look at the photos Jerrie sent, we relive that wonderful adventure again and again.

--Eddy Royeton

Birth, Life, Death, Infinity

I t was spring, 1991. I was the director of volunteers at a 26-bed AIDS hospice in Los Angeles. Many people would appear at my door keen to help those in their last six months of life. After a quick tour of rooms filled with wasted bodies and rattling breath, most prospective volunteers would reassess their altruism with nary a return phone call.

But then Brigid came to call, clad in Birkenstocks, a granny dress, and a corona of dried flowers. My nostalgia for the '60s was quickly replaced by profound skepticism as she produced a resume highlighting her work as a midwife and a healer.

Instead of blurting out, "A midwife in an AIDS hospice!" I asked her how she would apply her talents as a volunteer. "By birthing the dying and by helping to heal them of the sadness and regrets that hinder their passage," Brigid answered, her eyes serene as she met my bewilderment.

"How will you go about doing this?" I inquired, bewilderment changing to intrigue. "By sitting with them, merging our spirits, and accompanying them as they pass over." Intrigue returned to skepticism as I wondered if she were a jargon-spouting charlatan or a truly wise woman who somehow knew when death was imminent. She answered my thoughts. "If you still don't believe me after I've worked here for awhile, then you may invite me to leave. And, yes, I will know when my clients are ready to die."

After participating in the hospice orientation program, Brigid began. Or rather, the age of Brigid began.

I assigned her the angriest and most resistant residents whom Brigid visited regularly during the day. A licensed massage therapist, she would lay her hands on them or simply pass her fingers over their bodies. But it was during the night, a time when most residents died, that her true, intuitive kindness became apparent. Unerringly, Brigid appeared on the nights when her clients were released from life. She sat peacefully by their beds, joined her spirit with theirs, and journeyed with them down death's narrow corridor. The Guatemalan nursing aides, who all seemed to be most comfortable with the dying process, testified that when Brigid was present, the patients "departed like angels - their rooms glowed with light."

Brigid volunteered at the hospice for nine months. She and her life partner then departed for the Rockies, where, presumably, she continues to give birth to the living and the dying.

--Craig William O'Neill

Memories That Never Fade

I t is always so exciting when something we have accomplished is acknowledged and published either in the local newspaper, a magazine or even a monthly bulletin at work. The sad thing is that eventually the article fades, crumbles, or turns yellow.

For the past few years, I have been in the habit of cutting out articles I see written about people I know. I keep them in a folder and once a month I have them laminated. Then I send them to the individuals who are being acknowledged.

The laminated articles will not fade, crumble, or turn yellow and can be saved to admire and enjoy.

--Stephanie Hale

The Darkness Before the Light

I was at the sports medicine center with my mother waiting to see a doctor about my knee. An elderly lady came in, went to the desk, and was handed a stack of papers to fill out. She took the papers and sat down. After a bit, I noticed she was still on the first page.

She returned to the desk and asked the nurse if someone could help her fill out the papers as she was nearly blind. The nurse said she didn't have time to help and that the woman would have to make another appointment when she could bring someone with her to help.

I decided I would help her fill out the papers. I read the questions to her and wrote down her answers. I turned in the papers and told the lady good-bye.

As I was waiting in another room for the doctor, I heard the nurse put the elderly woman in a room down the hall. I wondered what caused her blindness, so I walked down to visit with her. She told me she had macular degeneration which would eventually cause complete blindness - there was no cure and nothing could help her. I knew this wasn't true.

You see, both my mother and my aunt have the same disease. Both are legally blind but, with the help of glasses developed by a doctor in Bakersfield, their eye sight is greatly improved. I then went to my mother and borrowed her glasses. The lady put them on. I handed her a paper with small print on it and she began to read it. When she was done, she started crying. She said she hadn't read for years.

I gave her the name of the doctor before I left. In a few brief minutes, I helped a person re-open a door that had been closed. I knew that lady would be able to read and write for years to come.

--Brenn Burtch

Food for Thought

While my girlfriend and I were grocery shopping, we started talking about her brother and his family. Things have been rough for them since he got hurt on the job. We decided to help them out with groceries and cut back half on what we would normally spend on our own.

The hard part was going to be getting the groceries into their home, as big brother doesn't like handouts from anyone. But I had an idea. I picked him up and brought him to my house for some advice on a room add-on, since he is a plasterer.

My girlfriend took the groceries to her brother's home. When I brought him back home, I thought his wife was going to hug me to death! He gave me a big hug and told me, "Thank you, brother, and you are my brother." I will never forget those words as long as I live. His wife was in tears the whole time - happy tears, at that.

--William Nutter

Do Unto Others

My husband, Dave, really has empathy for older people with disabilities. He had a friend who had Alzheimer's disease. As long as Harry was physically able, Dave took him to football games, local college basketball games and baseball games.

Now, every Sunday morning, Dave picks up a gentleman who is legally blind and takes him to church. After mass, they have breakfast at different local restaurants.

Even though all of these activities are things that Dave enjoys and would be attending anyway, he takes the time and effort to go that extra mile to make someone else's life more enjoyable.

--Nancy Blanco

Even An Angel Needs Kindness

T his story appeared in <u>The Bakersfield</u> <u>Californian</u> newspaper by Kern County Supervisor, Steve Perez. Steve wanted to share an act of kindness committed by firefighter, Jeff Van Andel, to show that there is still a lot of good that gets overlooked sometimes.

It began when a highway patrol officer stopped at the Keene Fire Station No. 11 and reported that a destitute motorist had been stranded in a disabled vehicle on Highway 58 for two days. He asked if there was anything the firefighters could do. Jeff Van Andel noticed the man appeared to be down on his luck. All of his possessions were in his beat-up van, including his upholstery business machines. The vehicle had a broken radiator hose and the man hadn't eaten in two days. Jeff invited him to eat lunch with them.

After lunch, Captain Maestas directed Van Andel to drive the stranded motorist to an auto parts store. En route, he noticed the man had a black eye and asked what had happened. He said he had come to California to work with his son in an upholstery shop. But things didn't work out and he was heading home to his beautiful wife. Somehow he made a wrong turn and was backtracking. Along the journey, he was assaulted when he attempted to stop a robbery.

At the auto parts store, Jeff noticed that the man only had $12 to pay for the radiator hose. He decided to give the stranger a $100 loan as it was apparent he didn't have enough money for the gas needed to go to Texas.

The firefighters helped the man put the radiator hose back on the van, filled up the radiator, and wished him good luck. Then Jeff phoned the man's wife to tell her he was on the road and would be home soon. He mentioned how much her husband missed her. The stranger's wife seemed surprised by the comments as she reported he was the one who left.

A couple of weeks later, Jeff Van Andel received a $100 certified check in the mail from Texas. The stranded motorist had a new job and was back with his wife. When asked why he loaned a complete stranger money, Jeff replied, "I know what it's like to be down and out in a situation like that. I also knew that he would pay me back. He was not a smooth talker. He was just a Texas farm boy, just like me."

On Christmas Day, the Keene fire station received a call from a man in Texas thanking them for their help when he was stranded in the area. He said he couldn't have made it without their assistance. The man only left his first name - *Angel*.

Walking the Walk

A friend shared her feelings about a recent shooting in a local parking lot. Two teenage boys had randomly shot and killed a 16-year-old girl and her boyfriend. My friend felt desperate. "We are no longer safe in our homes, shopping malls, schools, or cars," she said. She felt there was nothing we could do; "we're just hopeless victims."

Our conversation inspired me to establish *Because We Care*. I became involved in community efforts promoting kind acts as a way to improve the quality of life and to counter random acts of violence here. I produced a Random Acts of Kindness Calendar in 1994, printing suggestions for acts of kindness on certain days of the month.

Then in 1995, I visited third grade classrooms and spoke about the importance of being kind to each other. Students from each classroom wrote a brief story about a personal experience with an act of kindness. I selected 12 stories and printed them on our 1995 calendar. The stories were also sent to a teacher I made contact with in Okinawa, Japan. She shared these stories with her class and introduced the program to the school. They, in turn, wrote stories and sent them back to their "sister kindness class" in California.

A calendar for 1996 included photographs showing trust, sharing, gentleness, and kindness with stories. Sale of the calendars raised money for the Ronald McDonald House, where families of sick children stay while their youngsters receive treatment at a local hospital.

In 1995, we created Circles of Kindness. On Feb. 17, thirty-two schools gathered in their recreation centers at an assigned time, joined hands and formed "circles of kindness." That night, more than 100 gathered at city hall to celebrate Fresno's first Random Acts of Kindness Day with songs and flashlights. In 1996, we had the school children's circles again plus a poster contest about kindness.

Finally, school children from four schools made paper chains with acts of kindness written on each link. Four children from each school came to city hall where the chains were joined.

--Linda Lester

Merry Christmas, Emily

Being the single parent of 4-year-old Emily is never easy. But as that was my choice, I've always tried to do the best with what we have.

The holidays were upon us, the gas and electric company was on 15-day notice, and our special collection of Christmas ornaments had been lost in our last move. Merry Christmas, Emily.

During one particular conversation I had with my daughter's preschool director, Lisa Duncan-Purcell, I used her as a sounding board as I vented my frustrations. As I was about to discover later, she did more than listen. She took it all to heart.

The next week Lisa asked if Emily and I would enjoy being the recipients of some gifts from a woman who calls herself "Santa's Elves." I asked if there wasn't a family who needed it more. Lisa responded with, "No one deserves it more." That was the beginning of our Christmas.

The following few days brought an envelope. Enclosed were gift certificates to buy a tree and all the decorations. The note read, "...to restore your Christmas cheer." I thought that was the gift.

A few days before Christmas vacation, I was picking Emily up from school, when Lisa asked us to follow her out to the parking lot. The trunk of her car was bursting with beautifully wrapped packages, all bearing the name Emily.

Christmas came and my daughter's face became a constant reflection of pure joy. Showered in gifts that never before made it off the "wish list," Emily's memorable experience was one comparable only to that of a story book.

This woman, known only as Santa's Elves, has given us a gift more precious than any of the beautiful presents that lay under the tree. The idea that anyone would give so much to a family for no other reason than their own goodwill has restored the faith within me. Faith that there is good, that there is love and, most of all, that sheer kindness still exists.

Merry Christmas, Emily!

--Kristi A. Banks

Not Short Changed

M y mother was in a grocery store when the gentleman in front of her came up 20 cents short at the check out line. He assured the cashier that he must have 20 cents in his car and would go look for it. My mother reached in her purse and laid a handful of change on the counter and told the cashier to take whatever was necessary.

It seemed like a small act, but the gentleman was overwhelmed. He went on and on about how nice she was and that he was going to buy her a soda at the local soda fountain. Of course, he never bought her a soda, but my mother still smiles every time she thinks about how much that gentleman appreciated a gift of 20 cents.

--Lynda Stroud

Reach Out and Touch Someone's Life

O ne Sunday afternoon, Connie Money heard her 6-year old son answer the telephone and tell the caller that no one by the name of Mary lived there. After the same person called twice more in a short period of time, Connie told her son she would answer the next call.

The phone rang and Connie picked it up, repeated the same message her son had given earlier, but then went one step further. Connie recognized the voice as that of an elderly woman and asked how she had gotten her phone number. The caller, Mary, explained she was telephoning from another city and information had given her the number. She was trying to reach an old friend who had lost her son in the Viet Nam War. It was Mother's Day and Mary knew her friend needed to hear from someone who cared.

Connie asked Mary if she had an address for her friend. Upon hearing it was only a short distance from her home, Connie asked for Mary's number, told her she would go to her friend's home, let her friend know about the attempts to reach her, and give her Mary's phone number.

When Connie arrived at Mary's friend's home and explained her mission, the woman was extremely thankful and offered Connie her hospitality. Connie thanked the woman, excused herself, and said she simply wanted to deliver the message.

For most of us a wrong number is a nuisance. For Connie, it was an opportunity to give someone a hand.

Once when I walked home from the youth center, someone's cat was out in the rain. So I took it home. The next day, its owner came. I gave it back. I was 9 years old. Now that's a random act of kindness!

--Sean

To Repay Kindness

T he first kindness I can remember occurred when I was just a little boy. I lost a nickel, my bus fare home, and the owner of the fruit store where my mom shopped gave me a nickel. That was more than 50 years ago, but I still remember his kindness.

A few years later, the great Olympic Coach, Bob Alexander, was selecting members for the Boys Club swim team. At the end of the tryout, he announced everyone had made it. Based on the way I swam at the tryout, it was a kindness to allow me on the team. Each kind and each unkind act helps to form your personality and your perception of the world.

During my first career as a musician, I played without charge at many hospitals and nursing homes. In my second career in the insurance business, I have remained active volunteering in my professional organizations as well as in community work.

At the 1985 annual meeting of the Million Dollar Round Table in Dallas, I saw a presentation about the Make-a-Wish Foundation, which fulfills the special wishes of children with life threatening illnesses. We were told if there was no Make-a-Wish Foundation in our area, organize one. So I became the founder and first president of The Make-a-Wish Foundation of Hudson Valley, New York. Hundreds of children have had their wishes granted as a result of that chapter. But I wasn't the only member in that audience of 5,000 who was touched by that presentation. There were 17 other MDRT members who began chapters in communities throughout our nation as well as Australia, Canada, Brazil, England, and Japan.

In 1994, I was involved in planning the main platform for the Million Dollar Round Table annual meeting. We wanted to feature a worthwhile charity, just as Make-a-Wish had been featured in 1985. Habitat for Humanity was one of the charities we were considering. It occurred to me that if we could get volunteers from the MDRT to build a habitat home in Dallas, it would be a great way to say we believed in the project. We needed 39 volunteers to build a home. We thought we might have some difficulty getting that many people to take four days out of their lives, as well as the money to pay for their own travel, food, and lodging. By word of mouth, the volunteer slots were filled before we could request help The house was built. We filmed it and showed that as part of the presentation. In 1995, 18 more habitats were built throughout the United States with direct participation from MDRT members.

I have spent my life trying to repay kindnesses I have received. Each time I try to give something back, I become more blessed. It seems to be a universal truth, the more you give, the more you get.

--Steve Blake

Homeless and Hungry

T hough it was over 95 degrees outside, he was wearing jeans and an old flannel shirt. He was underweight and sat with his head down. In his hand was a sign that read "Homeless and Hungry. Please Help."

This was not the first time I had seen this man sitting on the corner. In fact, I had driven past him on many occasions and said to myself, "Why doesn't this lazy bum get a job?" However, this time, I turned my car around and headed to Wendy's. I ordered the largest meal possible, complete with a hamburger, French fries, and a large soda.

When I returned to the parking lot, I had a nervous feeling in my stomach. As I approached the man, my heart began to pound. He did not lift his head at my arrival. "Excuse me, sir," I said weakly. "You look hungry and I wanted to buy you a meal." He regarded me suspiciously, but as I handed him the bag of food, his eyes softened. "Thank you, miss," he said, "and may God bless you."

--Alison Martinez

Lighting the Way

F or more than 13 years, I have been a volunteer with the Connecticut Chapter of the American Liver Foundation. Many times I never meet the people I help by telephone, but, in other instances, some have become like family.

One such woman, Carol, without my knowledge, nominated me for the honor of being a Community Hero. A certified letter from the Atlanta Committe for the Olympic Games informed me I had been selected to carry the Olympic Torch on its run through Connecticut.

Imagine my joy and pride! For one-half mile, I ran as a once-in-a-lifetime part of history, carrying the flame proudly as it made its way to Atlanta for the 1996 games. My random act of kindness to a stranger was returned many times over. Forget Roger Banister's 4-minute mile. I wanted my incredible high to never end.

How wonderful it would be if a torch of kindness could be passed from one American to another across this great country of ours and then continue on to light the world!

--Bonnie K. Goldberg

THE END
(or just the beginning)

103D CONGRESS
2D SESSION

H. RES._____

IN THE HOUSE OF REPRESENTATIVES

MR. TUCKER SUBMITTED THE FOLLOWING RESOLUTION, WHICH WAS REFERRED TO THE COMMITTEE ON FEBRUARY 8, 1994

RESOLUTION

EXPRESSING THE SENSE OF THE HOUSE OF REPRESENTATIVES THAT THE PEOPLE OF THE UNITED STATES SHOULD BE ENCOURAGED TO PRACTICE RANDOM ACTS OF KINDNESS.

WHEREAS THE INCIDENCE OF RANDOM ACTS OF VIOLENCE IN THE UNITED STATES HAS REACHED EPIDEMIC LEVELS;

WHEREAS THE SURGEON GENERAL OF THE UNITED STATES ESTIMATES THAT, EVERY DAY IN THE UNITED STATES, 135,000 CHILDREN CARRY GUNS TO SCHOOL;

WHEREAS, EVERY DAY IN THE UNITED STATES, 3 CHILDREN ARE KILLED BY CHILD ABUSE, 9 CHILDREN ARE MURDERED, 13 CHILDREN ARE KILLED BY GUNS, 30 CHILDREN ARE WOUNDED BY GUNS, 307 CHILDREN ARE ARRESTED FOR CRIMES

OF VIOLENCE, 7,945 CHILDREN ARE REPORTED ABUSED OR NEGLECTED, AND 5,703 TEENAGERS ARE VICTIMS OF VIOLENT CRIME;

WHEREAS EVERY 4 HOURS A CHILD IN THE UNITED STATES COMMITS SUICIDE;

WHEREAS, IN THE UNITED STATES, EVERY 6 MINUTES A RAPE IS COMMITTED, AND EVERY YEAR BETWEEN 3,000,000 AND 4,000,000 WOMEN ARE BATTERED BY THEIR PARTNERS AND MORE THAN 200,000 WOMEN ARE STALKED;

WHEREAS, EVERY YEAR IN THE UNITED STATES, THERE ARE 4.7 RANDOM ACTS OF VIOLENCE COMMITTED AGAINST EVERY 1,000 PERSONS 65 YEARS OF AGE OR OLDER;

WHEREAS, EVERY YEAR IN THE UNITED STATES, THERE ARE 758.1 RANDOM ACTS OF VIOLENCE FOR EVERY 100,000 PERSONS IN THE UNITED STATES, AND 235 FIREARM-RELATED ACTS OF VIOLENCE FOR EVERY 100,000 PERSONS IN THE UNITED STATES;

WHEREAS, THERE ARE 238,000,000 HANDGUNS IN THE UNITED STATES;

WHEREAS, IN 1992 IN THE UNITED STATES, THERE WERE 1,730 ANTI-SEMITIC INCIDENTS, THE TOTAL NUMBER OF WHITE-SUPREMACIST GROUPS ROSE 27 PERCENT ABOVE THE NUMBER FROM THE PREVIOUS YEAR, AND A RECORD NUMBER OF

BIAS-RELATED   INCIDENTS,   INCLUDING   31
MURDERS, WERE REPORTED;

WHEREAS HATE CRIMES AGAINST ASIANS COMPRISED
8.9 PERCENT OF ALL HATE CRIMES DOCUMENTED
IN LOS ANGELES COUNTY IN 1990;

WHEREAS THE UNITED STATES STRONGLY OPPOSES
RANDOM ACTS OF VIOLENCE, AND ALL FORMS OF
INTOLERANCE AND MEAN-SPIRITEDNESS BASED
ON ETHNICITY, RELIGION, RACE, GENDER, OR
SEXUAL ORIENTATION; AND

WHEREAS DR. CHARLES WALL OF BAKERSFIELD
COMMUNITY COLLEGE HAS COMMITTED HIS
EFFORTS TO PROMOTING RANDOM ACTS OF
KINDNESS AMONG ALL PEOPLE: NOW, THEREFORE,
BE IT

RESOLVED, THAT IT IS THE SENSE OF THE HOUSE
OF REPRESENTATIVES THAT THE PEOPLE OF THE UNITED
STATES SHOULD BE ENCOURAGED TO PRACTICE RANDOM
ACTS OF KINDNESS, IN THE SPIRIT OF COMPASSION,
KINDNESS, AND GOODWILL TOWARD ALL PERSONS.